GREAT AMERICAN ◁ FOR JAMES BEARD AND JULIA CHILD, WHO LIT THE LAMP AND SHOWED US THE WAY ▷ COOKING SCHOOLS

GREAT AMERICAN COOKING SCHOOLS

Cooking from a Country Kitchen

SUZANNE TAYLOR

ILLUSTRATED BY MARC ROSENTHAL

IRENA CHALMERS COOKBOOKS, INC. • NEW YORK

*To Samuel Taylor, my chief taster and severest critic
and favorite kitchenmaid*

IRENA CHALMERS COOKBOOKS, INC.

PUBLISHER
Irena Chalmers

Managing Editor
Jean Atcheson

Sales and Marketing Director
Diane J. Robbins

Series Design
Helene Berinsky

Cover Design
Milton Glaser
Karen Skelton, *Associate Designer*

Cover Photography
Matthew Klein

Editor for this book
Jean Atcheson

Typesetting
Acu-Type Services, Clinton, CT

Printing
Lucas Litho., Inc., Baltimore

Editorial Office
23 East 92nd Street
New York, NY 10028
(212) 289-3105

Sales Office
P.O. Box 988
Denton, NC 27239
(800) 334-8128 or
(704) 869-4518 (NC)

ISBN #0-941034-17-8
©1983 by Suzanne Taylor. All rights reserved.
Printed and published in the United States of America
by Irena Chalmers Cookbooks, Inc.

LIBRARY OF CONGRESS
CATALOG CARD NO.: 83-071037
    Taylor, Suzanne.
        Cooking from a country kitchen
    New York, N.Y.: Chalmers, Irena Cookbooks, Inc.
84 p.

E D C B   6 5 4 3   695/15

Contents

Introduction

A cookbook is not a museum. Nothing is engraved in stone, not even your grandmother's favorite recipe. The truth about cookery is that we use everything we find in the past, anything we may discover in the present, and so provide for the future. Technique comes out of trial and error.

Times change, tastes change, our attitudes toward certain foods change, our eating habits change—and our ways of cooking change with them.

I grew up partly in America, partly in Norway and was partly educated in Switzerland. Good fortune has deposited me for some lengths of time in England and France and Italy, and my cooking reflects my varied background. In this book you will find a recipe for a fish chowder from New England, where I live now, and another for a fish chowder from my Norwegian grandmother. They differ, but they are good country cousins, alike in their respect for taste and simplicity. That is what good cooking is all about. Fresh fish, fresh meats, fresh fruits and vegetables treated with loving care are the foundation of good cooking everywhere.

I like living in my part of New England, way down on the rocky coast of Maine. Our house sits on a bluff at the head of the bay, looking out past the islands to the wide Atlantic. I always have the feeling on a clear day that if I looked hard I could see Spain on the horizon.

The quality of life here still has a satisfying simplicity. One can gather food as well as buy it. There is such pleasure in being able to pick wild blueberries and raspberries, dig clams at low tide and gather mussels from the seaweed-covered rocks. Smelts come upstream in April, the alewives in May. You can stand in the icy stream and catch them with your bare hands and toss them into a bucket. Mackerel fill the bay in July. On summer mornings as I eat my breakfast on the terrace, I can see the lobster boat circling around a few hundred feet out from shore. I hear the thud of the wooden traps as the lobsterman brings them aboard. If I hurry, I can catch him at the dock and pick up some lively lobsters for dinner.

It is no wonder that here, where I live, the feast of Thanksgiving is still the most beautiful and meaningful of all the American feasts. The foods have changed somewhat, and so have our ways of cooking them. But as the French say, "Plus ça change, plus c'est la même chose"; "The more things change, the more they are the same."

Consider the turkey. At the first Thanksgiving tables he graced, he was wild. With the passage of years he became domesticated, but still had the run of the barnyard. Our modern turkey, alas, has never touched ground. Never mind, things can be done. We cooks have learned a trick or two, over the centuries. The bird that graces our table today can still have splendor.

The great Brillat-Savarin, the philosopher of food, came to visit from France in 1794, and wrote with enthusiasm of a Thanksgiving dinner he ate in Connecticut. "A superb dinner," he said, "accompanied by excellent cider." He wrote of having partridge and squirrel as well as roasted wild turkey, and "two enormous pots of cider, of which I could not get enough." Hard cider, no doubt!

I know how he felt; cider is a lovely drink. In the early settlers' days it was the cheapest and the most abundant to be had, next to water. They drank it fresh, they drank it hard. In my part of the world they still do.

Thanksgiving marks the end of the long, legendary, color-bright autumn, days when you feel summer still lingering within your grasp, and you cherish each last flower and vegetable in your garden that has managed to escape the early frosts. A few remaining dark clusters of the fox-grape, which makes a delicious tart jelly, cling to the leafless vines. Opulent pumpkins, the Pasha of all the squash, lie heaped in a golden harvest, a reminder of pies to be made. At dawn, the timid deer steps warily into the apple orchard to eat the windfalls, and high overhead, geese fly in a great V formation, heading for winter quarters. Winter is about to descend on us, giving us time and the inclination to stay in a warm kitchen, try new recipes, and perhaps add some subtle changes to the old ones.

This New England that I live in is a place, but it is not a people—not anymore. Time has given us variety. It is true that you will find many names that recall those who came on

the *Mayflower* or followed close after, but very few of us now are descended from the ladies and gentlemen who stepped ashore from the high-prowed ships. We have come from many lands: France, Italy, England, Scotland and Ireland. And from Holland, Portugal, Norway, Sweden, Germany, Poland and Switzerland, to name just a few.

All those people who came to these shores in continuing waves brought with them the customs of the home lands and their own ways of preparing foods. Natural resources joined with national origins, and if the ingredients of the old country were lacking, the rich bounty of the new land supplied the necessary substitutes.

We are the richer for this. Over the years our cooking has been enhanced by new flavors, new concepts, a more varied approach to the preparation of food. New people still come in waves to our shores and America is discovered again and again. So is the art of cooking.

Some Quirks of My Kitchen

CRÈME FRAÎCHE

Crème fraîche has been a staple of French kitchens from time immemorial. Though called "fresh," it has a hint of sour to it, which gives dishes an added dash that sweet cream does not. Easily made at home (see page 46), it keeps for 10 days in the refrigerator. I always have some on hand to add to sauces and soups, or to garnish a fruit tart, or to spoon over the first ripe strawberries of the season.

EGGS AND CREAM

These two staples of cooking vary greatly, depending on where they are obtained. When I buy eggs from my neighboring farmer, some may be small young pullets' eggs, some almost as large as a duck egg. What the grocery store calls "extra large," to me is the normal-sized egg of my childhood.

I use the "extra large" in all recipes, such as cakes or custards, where eggs are a major part of the recipe, and I save my odd-sized fresh farm eggs for breakfast.

As for cream, I only use what is called "heavy cream," because the so-called "all-purpose cream" varies so much. Of course, if you want the old-fashioned heavy thick cream, you must find a friend with a nice Jersey cow, get a quart of unpasteurized milk and let it stand for 24 hours until the cream rises to the top. Then you will have something worth talking about—and cooking with!

FLOUR

Flours do differ, not only in the kind of wheat from which they are made, but in the milling process itself.

I once brought a small quantity of ordinary bread flour home from France, to test it against my American flour. The bread made with the French flour turned out a slightly coarser and springier loaf than the same recipe made with regular American flour.

For all my baking, unless a recipe specifically calls for cake or pastry flour, I use a regular brand of unbleached white flour. In any so-called white bread I make, I add a little whole wheat or rye flour, or even a little cornmeal, to give the bread the firmer texture I prefer.

"TRYING OUT" SALT PORK

Some people are puzzled by the expression "to try out salt pork." Small pieces—scraps, really—of salt pork are fried in a pan until they are brown and crisp. The fat is then poured off and used for frying; the scraps are drained on paper and are then ready to be used for added flavor in a stew or casserole and especially in a chowder.

This is very much a New England expression. I wonder if it is used in other parts of the country?

DRAINING SPINACH

Fresh spinach needs no more water for cooking than what clings to the leaves after really thorough washing. Even so, it is hard to drain. If you are going to cream the spinach, or even serve it plain with a little butter, all the moisture *must* be eliminated.

I turn the spinach first into a strainer to get rid of most of the water. Then, in order to get out every bit of moisture, I place the mass of cooked spinach on a large dinner plate, put another identical plate on top, right side up, so that they fit closely, and pressing the two plates together (over the sink), drain off the rest of the liquid.

CLEANING MUSHROOMS

If you have the patience to wipe each mushroom individually with a damp bit of rag, that is fine. But if expediency is the issue, place your mushrooms whole and dirty as they are in a plastic bag. Fill the bag with enough water to cover the mushrooms and add a tablespoon of flour. Now shake the bag vigorously, holding it over the sink. Empty the mushrooms into a strainer and dry them well. I find this much the best and quickest way to clean commercial mushrooms.

Recipes

FIRST COURSES

Every country has what the French term *hors d'oeuvres*, whether they are known as *antipasto* or *smørgås*, *Vorspeisen* or *zakuski*. The French, who always have more than one word for things, sometimes call them *amuse-gueule*, "amuse-the-mouth," which is nicely descriptive. The English call them "starters," which is basic, and we in America call them "appetizers," which is perhaps the best name of all, because the purpose of a first course is to titillate the appetite. You may serve a choice of dishes, or you may offer only one special thing: a small cheese croquette, a few stuffed mushrooms, or an artichoke vinaigrette.

As our eating habits have changed, and we pay more attention to caloric intake, the multicourse meals of an earlier day have almost entirely gone the way of calling cards and finger bowls, damask napkins and discreet black-uniformed maids. But when I am cooking dinner for friends, I like to serve a first course before the entree, to make the meal more of an occasion.

I choose my first course carefully: A Tomato Salad Mimosa (page 20), not too filling and so eye-appealing, or Smoked Haddock Mousse (page 14), in a dainty custard cup. If the main course is simple, say, a pot roast, or cold chicken with salad, I may indulge my guests with Blini and Red Caviar (page 19) to start, or a creamy soup, or my own pâté (page 16).

The beauty of these first courses is that each can be used as the principal dish for a simple luncheon, just by increasing the quantity and serving a vegetable or a salad or a slice of cold meat on the side. There are no borders when it comes to taste, so choose to serve what pleases you at the moment.

Smoked Haddock Mousse

Smoked haddock is fairly easy to come by. Most of it comes in from Canada, but if you're lucky, as I am, you may find a neighbor who smokes it for fun or profit and is willing to share. And then there is the true "finnan haddie" from Scotland, but we don't see much of that these days. If you can't get smoked haddock, try smoked fillets of cod or whiting. The important thing is that the fish be firm and have flavor.

This is a simple dish, and attractive, particularly if it is served in small individual crocks or ramekins. I like to serve it as a first course for a party. A small portion suffices, and it is light and tasty. It is also good as a light lunch dish, served with a sliced tomato and cucumber salad.

½ pound smoked haddock fillet
Milk, and water, for poaching
2 hard-boiled eggs
½ teaspoon grated onion
Dash of Worcestershire sauce
1 tablespoon unflavored gelatin
2 10-ounce cans beef broth or
**   bouillon (no gelatin added)**
½ cup heavy cream, whipped
Mayonnaise and chopped parsley,
**   for garnish**

Poach the haddock in half milk, half water for 8 to 10 minutes. Remove any skin or bones and flake the fish very finely. Discard the liquid. Chop the hard-boiled eggs finely and combine with the flaked haddock and the grated onion. Add a dash of Worcestershire sauce and set it aside.

Soften the gelatin in a little of the broth and bring the rest of the broth in a saucepan to a boil. Stir the softened gelatin into the heated broth, stirring well until it dissolves, then set aside to cool. When the broth is cool (but don't let it stiffen), add ⅔ cup of it to the haddock-egg mix. Fold in the whipped cream. Spoon this mixture into individual containers or a large serving dish, and refrigerate until completely set.

When the mousse is completely firm, pour cool, but still liquid jellied broth over the surface to a thickness of ½ inch and return to the refrigerator to set. Garnish just before serving with a small spoonful of mayonnaise and a little chopped parsley.

NOTE: You will probably have some broth left over to use in future soups or sauces.

Potted Shrimp

The shrimp caught off the coast of Maine are small and fickle. Sometimes they will be gathered abundantly for two or three years, only to disappear completely until the fancy strikes them to visit our shores once more. So, while we eat them fresh, we also preserve them as best we can, never knowing when there will be a further supply.

Any shrimp, anywhere, can be done this way.

Potted shrimp will keep in the refrigerator for a week to 10 days. They can also be frozen.

1 pound fresh small shrimp, peeled
20 tablespoons (2¼ sticks) unsalted butter
½ teaspoon salt
Pinch of white pepper
¼ teaspoon dried parsley
¼ teaspoon dried tarragon
1 tablespoon finely chopped shallot, cooked in a little butter
Dash of Worcestershire sauce

Put the shrimp into boiling salted water, allow to boil up again, and cook for barely 2 minutes. Put the shrimp in a strainer and immediately run cold water over them. Drain well and spread on paper towel to dry. Chop the shrimp into ¼-inch pieces.

Melt the butter in a small saucepan over low heat and add the salt, pepper, parsley, tarragon, cooked shallot and Worcestershire sauce. Stir to blend and allow to cool slightly. Pour over the shrimp and stir to mix well.

When the mixture begins to harden, give it a final stir to blend the shrimp evenly with the flavored butter, and pack into small jars. Keep in the refrigerator, or freeze until needed.

Serve cool, but not too cold, in small mounds on individual plates, with fingers of freshly made toast to spread.

Cold Roast Duck, Stuffed with My Own Pâté

There is a place on our coast where the Androscoggin River empties into the Gulf of Maine, called Merrymeeting Bay. It is a harbor where wild ducks, flying south in the autumn, pause to rest and feed. With hunters lying in wait, some will never reach their destinations, but will end up on a dinner table. I don't shoot, but I am happy when a friend who does brings me a brace of wild duck in the fall, especially if the birds have been cleaned and plucked, and are ready for the oven.

There is not an awful lot of meat on any duck, and so I like to extend the bird, be it wild or a plump domestic duckling, by roasting it and serving it cold, stuffed with my own pâté. It makes an elegant first course for a festive dinner. A small wild duck, even extended my way, will still only give three or four small portions. A four- or five-pound domestic duck makes a first course for six. And since the preliminaries for a festive dinner can sometimes get pretty frantic, I make it the day before.

DUCK

**A 4- to 5-pound domestic duck or
   two 2- to 3-pound wild ducks**
½ lemon
Salt and pepper
1 large onion, peeled
Pâté (see following recipe)
Olives or truffles, for garnish

Preheat the oven to 350 degrees.

Rub the duck well all over with the half lemon, sprinkle with salt and pepper and place the onion in the cavity. Place the duck on a rack in a shallow roasting pan and roast in the preheated oven for 1½ hours, or until tender.

Remove the duck from the oven, prick the skin all over with a fork, increase the heat to 450 degrees and return to the oven for another 15 minutes to brown, and for the fat to ooze out. (If you are using wild duck, after preparing the lemon, onion and seasoning, cover the breasts with slices of pork fat and roast 45 minutes in a 425-degree oven. Omit the pricking and defatting step, because the duck will be much leaner.) Remove to a platter and cool to room temperature.

To assemble: Using a sharp knife, cut along the breastbone and pull each half breast of the duck away from the bone, making two pockets. Stuff each pocket with pâté and reshape to form a plump duck breast. Cover the slit down the bone by decorating with sliced, pitted olives, or if you feel extravagant, sliced truffles. Carve the duck by cutting it in 1-inch slices crosswise, on a slant. Each serving should be partly pâté and partly duck.

PÂTÉ

2 tablespoons unsalted butter
**2 tablespoons finely chopped
   shallots**
2 tablespoons peanut or corn oil
**½ pound chicken livers, plus the
   duck liver**
Salt and pepper to taste
**3 tablespoons brandy or
   applejack**
½ teaspoon dried tarragon
2 ounces cream cheese
2-3 tablespoons heavy cream

Heat the butter in a frying pan over very low heat, add the shallots and cook until wilted and translucent. Set aside.

Remove any small pieces of membrane from the livers, and if they are large, cut them in half. Add the oil to the butter remaining in the pan, add the livers, sprinkle them with salt and pepper, and sauté for 4 or 5 minutes over fairly high heat, shaking the pan now and then to avoid sticking. (The livers should still be slightly pink inside.) Heat the brandy to lukewarm, light it with a match and pour it, flaming, over the livers.

Remove from the heat and add the tarragon and

shallots. Turn the contents of the pan into a food processor or a blender, add the cream cheese and the cream, and blend to a smooth puree. Adjust the seasoning and allow to cool, covered, before filling the breast.

If you are serving it on its own, chill for as long as you like, but be sure to take it from the refrigerator at least ½ hour before serving.

NOTE: This pâté is also good by itself, served with crackers at cocktail time.

Tomatoes Copenhagen *(WITH EGG AND CHIVE FILLING)*   *Serves 6*

Tomatoes ripen late in our garden, and the season is not long. They are on the daily menu as long as they last and we use them in numerous ways; hot, as a vegetable, cold, in a variety of salads. They may also be stuffed with all manner of fillings. This is one of them.

6 medium-size ripe tomatoes
9 large eggs
6 tablespoons heavy cream
3 tablespoons finely chopped chives
12 anchovy fillets
3 tablespoons butter
Salt and pepper to taste
Watercress or lettuce leaves, for garnish

Cut a slice from the tops of the tomatoes, scoop out the insides, and turn upside down to drain. Break the eggs into a bowl, add the cream and blend well with a fork or whisk. Melt the butter in a heavy saucepan, turn the heat to low and put in the eggs. Cook them very slowly, stirring gently with a spoon, scraping the bottom of the pan as the eggs cook. As they begin to form soft lumps, add salt and pepper and stir in the chives. Remove the eggs from the heat while they are still soft, and cool slightly.

Fill the tomato shells, dividing the eggs evenly among them, and top each one with 2 anchovy fillets, crossed. Place the filled tomatoes on plates, ready to serve, and garnish with a small lettuce leaf or a sprig of watercress next to each tomato. (The eggs do not need to be kept warm, but they should be served at room temperature, not refrigerated.)

Cheese Savories

Friends living in Connecticut are third-generation Swiss, and completely Americanized in their way of living, but cheese is such an inherent part of their background that several of the old Swiss recipes, handed down from their parents and grandparents, are a predominant part of their menus.

One of these cheese dishes is particularly good — and versatile, for while they serve it as a first course, I find it also makes a satisfying main course for lunch. Just this, and a green salad. Small round ones can also be made to eat with cocktails. Spear each one on a toothpick.

4 tablespoons butter
5 tablespoons flour
1 cup milk
½ cup heavy cream
½ pound Emmentaler (Swiss) cheese, grated
3 eggs, separated
Salt and pepper
Dried bread or cracker crumbs
Fat for deep-frying
Tomato Sauce (see following recipe)

Melt the butter in a saucepan, blend in the flour, and gradually add the milk and cream, stirring well after each addition. Cook over low heat until smooth and thick. Remove from the heat, stir in the grated cheese and allow to cool slightly. Then stir in the 3 egg yolks and the salt and pepper. Pour the mixture into a lightly buttered flat pan or dish about 6 by 9 inches. Refrigerate until completely chilled.

When the mixture is cold and stiff, immerse the bottom of the dish for a moment in hot water, then turn the mixture out onto a board or table. Cut it with a knife into small oblongs or squares and form these with your hands into little croquettes. Heat the fat for deep-frying to 375 degrees Fahrenheit. Roll each croquette first in the lightly beaten egg whites, then in the crumbs, and fry quickly in the hot fat until dark brown. Drain on paper towel and serve immediately with tomato sauce.

(If you wish, the croquettes can be kept warm in the oven for up to 30 minutes, but do not let them lose their crispness.)

They should be quite dark brown and crisp on the outside, soft and runny inside when you bite into them.

TOMATO SAUCE

1 tablespoon olive oil
1 medium-size yellow onion,
   finely chopped
1 medium-size carrot, peeled and
   finely chopped
2 medium-size stalks celery, finely
   chopped
2 pounds fresh, ripe tomatoes,
   peeled, seeded and chopped, or
   a 32-ounce can Italian plum
   tomatoes, drained and chopped
   (reserve the juice)
1 clove garlic, finely minced
1 teaspoon dried basil
½ teaspoon oregano
Salt and pepper to taste

Heat the olive oil in a small pan over low heat, add the chopped onion, carrot and celery, and cook until soft but not brown. Put the chopped tomatoes into a saucepan and stir in the onion mixture. Add the garlic, basil and oregano, and cook slowly for about an hour, or until thickened, stirring now and then to prevent sticking at the bottom. If the sauce seems too thick, add a little of the reserved tomato juice. Adjust the seasoning and serve.

NOTE: This sauce is also good with pasta dishes.

Raised Buckwheat Cakes or Blini
(SMALL RUSSIAN PANCAKES)   *Serves 6 as a main dish, 8 as a first course*

Raised buckwheat cakes have been a standby in New England homes since Colonial days. In households where they were served every morning, slathered with molasses or maple syrup, a cup of the batter was always reserved to "rise" the next batch, without having to use fresh yeast.

I make them sometimes for Sunday breakfast, but I prefer them, with a slight variation and under a different name, as a lunch or supper dish. I don't know how the tastes of the present Russian regime run, but in the days of the czars, small buckwheat cakes, called blini, *were served with the finest black caviar. Genuine caviar is now so astronomically priced that it is outside most budgets; however, any smoked fish or red salmon roe ("caviar" to the general), served with plenty of sour cream, makes a good accompaniment to blini.*

1 tablespoon (1 packet) dry yeast
2 tablespoons warm water
½ teaspoon sugar
1 cup buckwheat flour
1 cup white all-purpose flour
2 eggs, lightly beaten
1 cup milk
1 cup water
4 tablespoons butter, melted
Pinch of salt
Extra butter for frying, and to
   pour over the cakes
1 cup sour cream
2 ounces red caviar, or
   smoked fish

Combine the yeast, 2 tablespoons warm water and the sugar to activate the yeast. Set aside for 5 minutes. Meanwhile, put the two kinds of flour in a mixing bowl, add the eggs, milk and water, and stir well with a whisk. Add the melted butter, a pinch of salt and the yeast mixture, and stir well. Cover and let stand, either in a warm place, or in another bowl of warm water for 1 to 1¼ hours.

Heat a griddle or skillet and butter it lightly. Cook the blini as you would small hotcakes, turning once. Arrange them on a warm platter and pour a little melted butter over. Serve a bowl of sour cream and the caviar (salmon roe) or smoked fish, separately.

NOTE: Beer goes with blini better than wine, as does a small nip of vodka to start you off.

Tomato Salad Mimosa   Serves 4-6

If you like to begin your meal with a salad, this is a good one, particularly if you are following it with a large roast or a richly sauced dish, and want something not too filling before your main course. It is also appealing to the eye with its contrasting colors of red, green and yellow.

2 cucumbers, peeled and thinly
   sliced
Salt, as needed
3 large, ripe tomatoes, thinly
   sliced
Vinaigrette Dressing (see
   following recipe)
2 hard-boiled eggs, yolks and
   whites finely chopped,
   separately
3-4 scallions, cleaned and finely
   chopped (using some of the
   green part), for garnish

Place the sliced cucumbers in a dish, sprinkle liberally with salt and allow to stand and drain for 20 minutes. Put the cucumber slices in a strainer and run cold water over them to eliminate the salt. Drain well, place on paper towel and pat dry.

Arrange the tomato and cucumber slices on a platter, alternating them in groups or slices, or as you wish. Pour over the vinaigrette dressing. Make alternate strips of egg yolk and egg white on top of the tomato and cucumber, and decorate around the edge of the platter with chopped scallions.

VINAIGRETTE DRESSING

3 tablespoons olive oil
1 tablespoon wine vinegar
½ teaspoon Dijon mustard
4 or 5 drops of heavy cream
Salt and pepper to taste

Mix all the ingredients in a small bowl with a whisk, adding the cream last and blending it in well. Adjust the seasoning.

Pepper Cheese Puffs

Serves 6-9

These are mouth-wateringly delicious, and people find it hard to guess exactly what they are made of, which is always fun for the hostess. The unusual use of whipped egg whites in this way conceals the contrasting filling and binds everything together. From the delighted remarks they evoke, these puffs are well worth the trouble of a little last-minute preparation—though, actually, they can be prepared almost entirely ahead. Only the whipping of egg whites and the spreading on of this topping must be done just before they are popped in the oven.

You can also make them in smaller rounds, or squares, and serve them with drinks.

6-8 slices of white bread
2 eggs, separated
⅓ cup finely minced fresh
   green pepper
1 cup grated cheddar cheese
¼ cup grated Parmesan cheese
Dash of Tabasco sauce
Pinch of salt

Toast the bread lightly and, using a 2½-3-inch cutter, or a glass, cut a neat round out of each slice. Discard the crusts.

Blend the 2 egg yolks, green pepper and the cheeses in a bowl. Add (carefully!) a dash of Tabasco and blend it in well. Whip the egg whites in a separate bowl with a pinch of salt until they form soft peaks. (Do not overbeat, or it will be difficult to spread them.)

Preheat the oven to 400 degrees.

Pile the cheese mixture onto the toast rounds, heaping it slightly in the center of each. Cover each piece all over with whipped egg whites, like a meringue. Put the prepared toasts on a cookie sheet and bake for 8 to 10 minutes, or until the topping takes on a nice tan color. Serve immediately while hot.

SOUPS

Soups fall into two categories. One is the soup you serve at the start of a meal, the other is a meal on its own. I love them both.

A soup that begins a meal should take into consideration the dishes that follow. Serve a light soup before a heavy meal; serve a soup with more body if it is to be followed by a soufflé or a salad. A hearty soup makes a satisfying lunch all by itself, particularly if you've been out in winter weather.

Few of us these days have a perpetually simmering stockpot on the back of the wood stove (although it seems we may be coming back to it). I regularly save for stock all the chicken carcasses and bones from a roast, as well as vegetable peelings or that extra carrot and turnip cluttering up the vegetable bin. If I have none of these at hand, I buy fresh chicken backs, necks or wings from the butcher and make a strong, pure chicken stock that I keep in the refrigerator for my needs. It keeps well for a week. If it is not all used up in that time, I reboil what's left for a few minutes, or freeze it in ice cube trays or in a pint plastic container.

If you have no stock and no time to make any, a good brand of canned chicken broth or beef bouillon makes an adequate substitute, though I do find the bouillon flavor tends to overpower the other ingredients. A little sherry, or Madeira (which I prefer), added to a clear bouillon can lift it out of the ordinary.

Blenders and food processors have opened up endless possibilities for ever-new thick soups. A few vegetables from the garden, some stock or broth and the proper seasonings — and you have an infinite variety of soups with a few twirls of your machine.

Leek and Potato Soup

The French think they invented it, and call it Potage Parmentier. *The Americans, with their hot summer days, serve it cold and call it* Vichyssoise. *I just call it Leek and Potato Soup. I serve it hot or cold, depending on the weather, and any day it is one of my favorites.*

4 leeks, white part only
5 tablespoons unsalted butter
1 small onion, thinly sliced
5 cups chicken broth, homemade or canned
4 medium-size potatoes
¼ teaspoon mace
½ teaspoon freshly grated nutmeg
Salt and pepper to taste
1 cup milk
½ cup heavy cream

Trim the leeks and wash them thoroughly, splitting them through to the center to eliminate any sand or grit. Cut them across into 1-inch pieces. Heat 3 tablespoons of the butter in a heavy pan, add the leek and onion and cook over low heat until soft. Do not allow the vegetables to brown. Pour in the chicken broth and simmer for half an hour. Meanwhile, peel the potatoes and boil in salted water until soft.

When all the vegetables are cooked, force them through a strainer or food mill into a large saucepan and add the chicken broth and the seasonings. Stir in the milk and bring the mixture to a boil, then reduce the heat. Stir in the rest of the butter and the cream, adjust the seasoning and serve piping hot.

NOTE: If the soup is to be served cold, chill it well and garnish each cup with a little chopped chives.

Blender Borscht *(BEET SOUP)*

Borscht is basically a Russian or Polish soup, and it comes with many variations. Some recipes call for cabbage and potatoes, others for tomatoes and a touch of vinegar, but the principal ingredient is always—beets. I have tried all these recipes on my ultimate taster, my husband. He claims to prefer this simple borscht, quickly made in the food processor, to all the others.

4-5 medium-size beets, boiled and peeled
4 cups beef broth, homemade or canned
1 tablespoon lemon juice
Salt and pepper to taste
4 heaping tablespoons sour cream and
4 sprigs of fresh dill, to garnish each cup

Cut the beets into quarters and process until finely pureed. Gradually add 1 third of the broth to the beets in the food processor, along with the lemon juice, salt and pepper. Transfer to a saucepan, stir in the remainder of the broth and bring almost to a boil over moderate heat. Taste for flavor and consistency, adding more broth if you find the soup too thick. It may be served hot or cold. Be sure to garnish each cup before serving with a generous spoonful of sour cream and top with a sprig of fresh dill.

Suzy's Soup

A concoction of my own, this is a delicate, savory soup that wakes up the taste buds, leaves them fresh for the rest of the meal, and is not too filling. It is an ideal summer soup here in Maine, or, for that matter, anywhere where fresh crabmeat can easily be found. I've never made it with frozen or tinned crab, but I should think it would be worth the try if fresh crab is not handy.

The nutmeg is important, and must be freshly grated. Nutmeg that is grated ahead of time loses its flavor and tastes like sawdust.

1 tablespoon unsalted butter
1 tablespoon finely chopped
   shallot
½ pound fresh crabmeat
4 cups chicken broth, homemade
   or canned
8-10 fresh spinach leaves
¼ teaspoon freshly grated nutmeg
Salt and pepper to taste

Heat the butter in a heavy pan and add the chopped shallot. Cook over gentle heat until soft, but not brown. (The French describe this brief cooking as to *fondre*, or "melt" the shallots or onions, a very apt expression.)

Add the crabmeat to the pan with the shallots. Mix and stir over low heat for a minute or two. Put the chicken broth into a good-sized pot, heat, add the spinach leaves and bring to a boil for 2 or 3 minutes, just long enough to wilt the leaves. Remove the spinach with a slotted spoon, chop coarsely and add to the pan containing the crabmeat. Stir the spinach into the mixture and season with nutmeg, salt and pepper to taste.

Divide the crabmeat-spinach mixture among the soup bowls, top with piping-hot chicken broth and serve immediately.

Scandinavian Fish and Vegetable Chowder

Serves 6-8

I first met this chowder in Norway, where fish of many varieties are taken from those cold, Nordic waters. The Scandinavians make a chowder that is less starchy than ours; no potatoes, no crackers, but with fresh vegetables cooked in it.

3 pounds fresh cod or haddock
12 whole peppercorns, preferably
  white
1 bay leaf
1 tablespoon chopped parsley
4 medium-size carrots, cut into
  1-inch pieces
8 small white onions, cut in half
1 small head of cauliflower,
  separated into florets
1½ cups water
2½ cups milk, scalded
1 cup light cream
Pinch of cayenne pepper
Salt to taste
1 tablespoon chopped fresh chives

Set the whole piece, or pieces, of fish in a big stockpot and add enough salted water to barely cover it. Add the peppercorns, bay leaf and parsley, and bring to a boil. Reduce the heat and simmer until the fish comes away easily from the bone.

Take the fish out of the pot, saving the stock, and remove all skin and bones. Flake the fish into fairly large pieces and set aside. Boil down the reserved fish stock to reduce by half.

Meanwhile, put the carrots, onions and cauliflower in a pot with 1½ cups of water. Boil for 5 minutes, then add both the vegetables and the cooking water to the reduced fish stock in the stockpot. Add the scalded milk, the cream and the pinch of cayenne, and salt according to taste.

Put the flaked fish back into the pot with the other ingredients and heat well. Before serving, garnish with chopped chives.

Old-Fashioned New England Fish Chowder

Serves 6-8, depending on how many come back for more

People who live by the sea make chowders. That is a univeral truism. There is no country in the world that I know of, with a seacoast, that does not have its own chowder or hearty fish soup. And they are always "a-meal-in-itself-and-come-back-for-more."

Old-fashioned New England Fish Chowder is one of my favorites. Most recipes call for common crackers or pilot biscuits to be soaked in milk, or in the chowder, until soft. I prefer a handful of crisp, small oyster crackers, dropped into the bowl as the chowder is served.

2 pounds cod or haddock fillets
3 cups fish stock or clam juice
1 ounce fat salt pork, cut into small cubes
2 medium-size onions, thinly sliced
2 tablespoons flour
3 medium-size potatoes, cut into ½-inch cubes
4 cups milk, scalded
¼ teaspoon mace (optional)
Salt and pepper to taste
2 tablespoons unsalted butter
1 teaspoon chopped parsley

Poach the fish fillets gently in 1 cup of fish stock or clam juice for 4 to 5 minutes. Add a little water, if necessary. Set aside.

"Try out" (see page 9) the salt pork and set aside with the fish. Cook the sliced onions in the pork fat until soft and translucent, sprinkle with the flour and stir to blend. Gradually stir in 2 cups fish stock or clam juice, add the potatoes, and cook for 2 or 3 minutes over low heat. Add the scalded milk. Flake the fish and add it to the pot, along with its juice and the pork scraps. Season to taste. Add the butter, cut into small pieces, and serve the chowder hot in large individual bowls. Sprinkle a little parsley on each bowl before serving.

Quick and Easy Tomato Soup

Serves 4

This is a refreshing soup to serve on a hot summer day. The colors are appealing, especially if you can serve it in thin, white china cups.

4 cups tomato juice
1 tablespoon grated onion
1 cup light cream
Dash of Tabasco sauce (be careful!)
Salt and pepper to taste
½ cup sour cream
Chopped fresh dill for garnish

Mix the tomato juice, onion, cream, Tabasco, salt and pepper together in a mixing bowl. Chill for at least 2 hours. Just before serving, place about 1 heaping teaspoon of sour cream on top of each cup of soup, and sprinkle with chopped dill.

I serve my Thin Cornbread (see page 70) with this.

Two Sorrel Soups

I grow a lot of sorrel in my garden. Webster's Unabridged Dictionary, *composed in Connecticut, curtly dismisses sorrel as "a plant with sour juice." Ah, if Mr. Webster had only known! Or, more to the point, if Mrs. Webster had only known! There must have been wild sorrel growing in the fields around their Connecticut home. The plant thrives in our New England climate. It pushes its way up through the melting snows of March, and I have to fight the deer for the first tender shoots. The deer must find it a tonic, for they will steal in from the woods and come close to the house just to nibble it.*

I certainly find it a tonic, one of the loveliest I know. I use it all summer long for soups and for sauces and to pep up blander vegetables. I make a bed of it for poached salmon. Most often I make a soup of it. The two that follow are equally good. I like to make the richer one for parties.

Thomas Jefferson mentions in his journal buying "nice, fresh sorrel in the market." You don't often find it in the market, these days. You'd better grow it. It'll grow almost anywhere.

Simple Sorrel Soup *(POTAGE SANTÉ)*

1 large bunch of sorrel (I have never weighed sorrel picked from my garden, but ½ pound should be plenty)
1 tablespoon unsalted butter
1 tablespoon finely chopped onion
1 or 2 small carrots cut into 1-inch pieces
1 medium-size potato, peeled and boiled
4 cups chicken broth (homemade or canned)
Salt and pepper to taste
1 tablespoon finely chopped parsley for garnish

Wash the sorrel well in several changes of water. Cut off the stems and discard. Select a lidded saucepan big enough to hold the sorrel, melt the butter in it and wilt the onion, but do not brown. Add the sorrel leaves, cover the pot, and cook about 5 minutes until the leaves are wilted and no longer green. (The water that clings to the leaves after they have been washed should be enough to keep them from sticking to the pot, but if necessary, add a little stock. You may have to stir the leaves around so that all of them are wilted and brown.) While the sorrel is cooking, boil the carrots in water for 5 minutes.

Force the cooked carrots, potatoes and sorrel through a sieve, or puree them in a food processor. (I chop the vegetables in a food processor, but leave them quite coarse as I prefer the texture.) Add the vegetable puree to the chicken broth, bring to a quick boil and season with salt and pepper. Serve sprinkled with finely chopped parsley.

NOTE: If you find the soup too thick, add more chicken broth to thin it.

Cream of Sorrel Soup

1 large bunch of sorrel (about ¾ pound)
8 cups chicken broth
4 egg yolks
2½ cups cream (light or heavy, depending on your mood)
¼ teaspoon freshly grated nutmeg
Salt and pepper to taste
Freshly grated carrot (optional), for garnish

Wash the sorrel well in several changes of water. Discard the stems and put the sorrel leaves in a saucepan along with a little chicken broth. Wilt the leaves over moderate heat until they are no longer green. Puree the sorrel either through a strainer, or in a food processor.

Bring the remaining chicken broth to a boil in a large pot and stir in the pureed sorrel. Remove from the heat. Beat the egg yolks and the cream just until they are blended, then add the mixture to the broth. Stir in the nutmeg and season to taste with salt and pepper. Heat the soup carefully, continuing to stir, but do not let it boil. This soup should be smooth and creamy. I like to grate a little raw carrot on top of each bowl, for color contrast.

VEGETABLES

Many vegetables have been cultivated and developed through the years from their wild state, and different parts of vegetables serve different purposes. We eat the roots of carrots, turnips and beets, but the new young shoots of asparagus. We eat artichokes, whose origin lies in the bud of a thistle, the leaves of several kinds of cabbage and all the many leafy salad greens, and the flowers of broccoli and cauliflower. I grow chard in my garden. The large, crinkly green leaves are cooked as you would spinach, the broad white stalks, braised, are a look-alike for celery.

Smaller is better when it comes to garden vegetables. If you want to grow a mammoth blue-ribbon prize-winning pumpkin for the fair, that's one thing. But for eating, take the small early zucchini with its blossom still attached, the tiny crunchy carrots, and the stringlike beans, tedious to pick but so rewarding when eaten. All these are greatly prized by the French, who call them *les primeurs*, the beginnings, the first fruits of the burgeoning season. And later in the year, here in Maine after the potato harvest, to walk along a field and pick from the upturned furrows the walnut-sized potatoes, abandoned as too small for commercial use—here is real treasure.

Certain vegetables go well together. Sliced zucchini with cherry tomatoes, sautéed in butter and served with a roast, are pleasing contrasts in color as well as taste. Carrots and peas with small white turnips are a tricolor triumph. Even the much-maligned parsnip, boiled and "married" to mashed potatoes and properly seasoned, becomes an interesting side dish. What a profusion to choose from, not only for vegetarians, but for us all.

Covered Cauliflower

This is a very pretty dish. Do not let the top become too golden brown, because the charm of this recipe lies in the contrast between the pale green broccoli and the creamy white cauliflower, hidden from view—until you cut in and expose the layers.

1 medium-size head cauliflower
1 teaspoon salt
1 large bunch broccoli
2 tablespoons butter
¼ cup sour cream
½ teaspoon pepper
½ cup breadcrumbs
2 tablespoons freshly grated
   Parmesan cheese

Wash the cauliflower, break into florets and cook in salted water until tender but not mushy, about 15 minutes. Drain the cauliflower, but save the cooking water.

Wash the broccoli and break into florets. Peel the stalks down to the tender part and chop coarsely. Cook in the cauliflower water for about 8 to 10 minutes. Puree the cooked broccoli (in a food processor, if you have one) and add the butter, sour cream and pepper. Taste for salt.

Preheat the oven to 350 degrees.

Place the cauliflower florets in a lightly buttered baking dish. Spoon the broccoli puree over them, completely covering the white cauliflower. Sprinkle with breadcrumbs, then with grated Parmesan, and bake in the preheated oven for 25 minutes. Serve in the baking dish.

Hashed Brown Potatoes, Swiss Style (ROESTI)

This authentic national dish of Switzerland is a remarkably good variation on American hashed browns. The difference and the secret lie in the fact that the potatoes are cooked in two steps: in step 1, they are half-boiled and chilled, and in step 2, peeled, grated and sautéed until cooked through.

4 medium to large potatoes
4 tablespoons vegetable oil
2 tablespoons unsalted butter
Salt and pepper to taste

Scrub the potatoes and cook with the skins on for 10 to 12 minutes until partially cooked. Drain, cool and chill for several hours or overnight. When they are thoroughly chilled, peel them and shred on a coarse grater.

Heat most of the oil and the butter in a medium-sized omelette pan or heavy skillet. (It should be just big enough to hold the potatoes in a layer about an inch thick.) Add the shredded potatoes, sprinkle with salt and pepper, and cook over moderate heat, stirring occasionally, until the underside is brown and crusty. Reverse onto a plate, add more oil and butter to the pan, if necessary, then slide the potatoes back again into the pan to brown the other side. Give the pan a gentle shake, now and then, and peek at the underside to see if it is browning. Put on a platter, cut into wedge-shaped pieces, and serve. Cooking time in the pan should take about 30 minutes.

Potatoes with Onions and Cabbage *(COLCANNON)* *Serves 6*

This dish, invented by the Irish, makes good use of potatoes, with the addition of onions and cabbage. The Scots added carrots, but I prefer the Irish version. On a cold winter evening it makes a hearty one-dish meal when augmented by small pork sausages, their drippings poured over the mound of potatoes. It is claimed that potatoes in themselves are not fattening, so for the calorie-conscious, leave off the drippings. And since the vegetables are cooked in plain broth, let your caloric conscience rest easy.

1 small head cabbage
2 medium-size yellow onions
1 cup chicken or beef bouillon
   or broth (homemade or canned)
6 medium-size potatoes
2 tablespoons unsalted butter
¼ cup milk
Salt and pepper to taste
1 tablespoon finely chopped
   parsley
1 pound pork sausages (optional)

Cut the core out of the cabbage and cut the cabbage into 6 or 8 segments. Peel the onions and slice thinly. Cook the cabbage and onions in the bouillon for about 15 minutes, until soft. Drain the cabbage and onions, reserving the liquid.

Meanwhile, peel the potatoes, cut into quarters and boil in salted water until soft. Drain and mash them, adding the butter, milk, salt and pepper. Mix in ⅓ cup of the cabbage broth, or more, if you like a softer consistency. Add the cooked cabbage and onions and mix all well together. Mound on a heated platter and sprinkle with chopped parsley.

If you are defying calories, surround the mound of potatoes, cabbage and onions with cooked sausages, of whatever kind pleases you—from small breakfast sausages to the larger kielbasa (Polish) or pepperoni (Italian).

Parsnip and Potato Casserole

Serves 4-6

This is the only way I can get my husband to eat parsnips. Take care to use nice fresh ones for this dish; they should be no larger than medium-size carrots, to avoid the woody centers that come when they grow older.

4 medium-size potatoes
4 medium-size parsnips
3 tablespoons milk
2 tablespoons sherry or Madeira
3 tablespoons unsalted butter
2 eggs, separated
½ teaspoon freshly grated nutmeg
Salt and pepper to taste
Dry breadcrumbs for topping
Chopped parsley or watercress
** sprigs for garnish**

Scrub the potatoes but do not peel them. Boil in salted water until soft. Boil the parsnips until soft but not mushy. Peel the potatoes and parsnips and force them through a ricer or a food mill into a bowl. Add the milk and sherry or Madeira, 2 tablespoons of the butter, the egg yolks, nutmeg, salt and pepper, and stir all together to blend well. Adjust the seasoning to taste.

Preheat the oven to 375 degrees.

Whip the egg whites until they hold peaks, and fold them gently into the mixture. Turn the mixture into a lightly buttered baking dish, cover with breadcrumbs and dot with the remaining butter. Bake in the preheated oven for 35 to 40 minutes, or until the breadcrumbs become golden. Garnish with chopped parsley or sprigs of watercress.

Sautéed Zucchini and Cherry Tomatoes

Serves 6

The zucchini is prolific and popular in the summer garden, but should be picked while small. Beyond a certain size, they are only good when stuffed with something to give them body and flavor, or to be put in a soup pot along with more flavorful vegetables.

4 small (about 6-inch) zucchini
12-15 cherry tomatoes
1 clove garlic (2, if you like it)
2 tablespoons olive oil
Salt and pepper to taste
1 tablespoon chopped fresh basil
** or parsley for garnish**

Wash and dry off the zucchini and cut into 1-inch pieces. Remove the blossom end from the tomatoes and check to see that they are clean. Peel the garlic and chop finely. Heat the oil in a fairly large skillet and add the tomatoes, zucchini and garlic. Cook over moderate heat for about 5 minutes, or until soft, stirring with a wooden spoon or paddle to coat the vegetables with oil on all sides. Season with salt and pepper. Garnish before serving with chopped basil or parsley.

NOTE: This dish goes particularly well with Parsleyed Leg of Lamb (page 55).

Carrots Glebe House

In certain gardens in this area of Maine, June brings forth a profusion of tiny pale-pink roses covering very thorny bushes. Rosa spinosissima *was first brought here from Scotland by the parents of a neighbor, and some of us have been lucky recipients of offshoots. Our neighbor also shares with us a recipe named Carrots Glebe House in memory of the parsonage her parents left behind.*

3 large or 5-6 small carrots
3 small potatoes
2 small onions
1-2 cups chicken broth
1 teaspoon fresh thyme, or ½
** teaspoon dried**
⅓ cup heavy cream
Salt and pepper to taste
1 tablespoon finely chopped
** parsley**

Peel and dice the carrots. Peel the potatoes and cut them into quarters. Peel and dice the onions. Boil the potatoes in salted water until they can be pierced with a fork. Drain and set aside. Put the carrots and onions in a pot with enough chicken broth to cover, and cook until just soft. Pour off the remaining liquid and save to use in a vegetable soup.

Mash the carrots, onions and potatoes together with a potato masher, or put them through a ricer. (I never put potatoes through a food processor because I find it makes them slimy.) Add the cream, and salt and pepper to taste, mix well together and reheat over moderate heat. Sprinkle with parsley just before serving.

Tuna-Bean Salad

Some salads are served as a side dish, or as a separate course; others can stand alone as meals. This is one of the latter and makes a good, fairly substantial lunch dish. It may be garnished with olives or with strips of pimiento to give it color, or with quarters of hard-boiled eggs as an added attraction. Because dried beans have to be soaked, and cooked quite a long time (depending on the instructions on the package), this should be done several hours before the salad is needed.

¾ cup white pea beans
7-ounce can tuna, drained
2 stalks celery, chopped
3 scallions, chopped
Lettuce leaves
Olives, pimiento strips, or
    hard-boiled egg quarters,
    for garnish

MARINADE:
⅓ cup olive oil
2 tablespoons vinegar
1 teaspoon freshly squeezed
    lemon juice
½ teaspoon Dijon mustard
1 small clove garlic, crushed
    (optional)
Salt and pepper to taste

Prepare the beans according to the instructions on the package. Drain and allow to cool slightly. Make the marinade and pour over the beans. Allow to marinate for at least 30 minutes, turning the beans with a fork to coat them well.

Put the tuna in a bowl and break it up into bite-sized pieces. Add the beans and their marinade, and the celery and scallions. Mix well. Heap the tuna-bean mixture on a bed of lettuce leaves and garnish with sliced olives or pimiento or hard-boiled egg quarters, as desired.

Endive and Beet Salad

This is a simple but very pretty salad, good to serve as a side dish or as a separate course, perhaps with cheese and crackers.

Equal proportions of Boston, or
    other lettuce, Belgian endive,
    and sliced, cooked beets
Marinade, as needed (above)
Watercress for garnish

Make a bed of the lettuce in a salad bowl. Arrange the Belgian endive and the beets attractively on it, and pour the marinade over. Garnish with a few sprigs of watercress.

Potato-Green Bean Salad

This salad goes particularly well with cold sliced baked ham, or cold roast beef.

18 small new potatoes
½ cup Marinade (opposite page)
½ pound string beans
1 small onion, finely chopped
Salt and pepper to taste
3 medium-size ripe tomatoes,
  peeled and quartered
Chopped fresh dill or parsley
  for garnish

Scrub the potatoes and boil in salted water until cooked—they should be firm, not mushy. Drain, and cut into halves or quarters, according to their size. Do not peel. Put into a bowl, pour the marinade over while they are still warm, and leave to marinate for 30 minutes.

Boil the string beans just until they begin to soften—they should still be crisp, not limp. Drain them in a strainer and run cold water over them to stop the cooking. Set aside to cool.

Combine the potatoes and their marinade, the string beans and the chopped onion in a bowl. Taste and adjust seasoning. Arrange the salad on a platter or in a shallow bowl, surround with quartered tomatoes and sprinkle dill or parsley over the top.

Coleslaw

This was originally a German dish, in which the cabbage was cooked, whereas we think of coleslaw as being a salad made with uncooked cabbage. The name derives from kohl (cabbage) and "slaw," the old English word for salad. This recipe differs from most, as there is no sugar in it, but the addition of carrots does sweeten it slightly. I also add caraway seeds, that ubiquitous northern condiment, for this recipe is of Norwegian derivation. It is especially good as a side dish with shellfish or any seafood, and in our house a must *with lobster.*

1 medium-size head cabbage
1 large or 2-3 small carrots
1 tablespoon grated onion
2 tablespoons olive oil mixed with
  1 tablespoon vinegar
Salt and pepper to taste
1 cup mayonnaise
1-2 tablespoons caraway seed,
  according to taste

Cut out the core of the cabbage and shred the leaves finely. Peel and shred the carrots. Put the cabbage and carrots in a large mixing bowl and add the onion, olive oil and vinegar, and salt and pepper. Mix all well together with a large fork. Gradually add the mayonnaise, continuing to mix with the fork. (You may not need the whole cup as this salad should not be too moist.) Scatter the caraway seeds over and mix them in well. Chill the salad before serving.

FISH AND SHELLFISH

Anyone who has lived near enough to the sea or to a lake or stream to catch his own fish, or who has had access to a harbor where fishermen sell their catch directly from their boats, is forever spoiled for anything less.

In the Norwegian coastal town where I spent a good part of my childhood summers, I often went with my grandfather to the cobblestoned market square where dozens of fishing boats, just in from the sea with their catch, were tied up. The boats lay low in the water, their open cockpits full to the gunwales with a seething, silvery mass of very lively fish. The fish for sale were displayed on rough wooden stands, set up on the edge of the pier above the boats, and from time to time a few fish would be tossed up from below to replenish the rapidly emptying stands.

It would not have entered my grandfather's head to make any of the other household purchases—that was women's work. But my grandmother and her cook relied entirely on his practiced eye to select only the finest, freshest fish. He would have turned up his nose at the re-frigerated fish that passes as fresh in most of our markets. Today, I would rather eat the humblest of fish, Monk-fish, known to fishermen as "trash fish," as long as it was alive and well when I first looked it in the eye. For grandfather taught me that a fish's eye should be bright and shining, not dull and glazed. The gills should be a nice fresh red, and the fish itself firm but resilient to the touch.

Unfortunately, most of the fish sold in Maine these days, instead of being sent to market directly from where they are landed, go to the big Boston fishmarket and then are shipped back to Maine by truck. So the pound of haddock I paid so dearly for was undoubtedly caught several days earlier. It is ironic that in a state with a reputation for seafood, it is difficult to go to market and buy truly fresh fish. On the other hand, we are fortunate to have the freshest of shellfish right at our doorstep: mussels for the picking, clams to be dug, fresh scallops and tiny shrimp in the long winter season, and lobsters and crabs all summer long.

"The sea hath fish for every man" went the 16th-century saying—and while this may well have been allegorical, certainly in earlier days our coastal waters were teeming with fish. Alas, pollution and overfishing have taken a terrible toll. We still can get the beautiful Atlantic salmon that used to be so plentiful, but it is harder to come by. In our part of New England, we celebrate our independence with a traditional Fourth of July dinner: fresh salmon and the first peas of the season. I hope we never have to forego this pleasant custom.

Boiled Lobster, Plain and Simple

Count a 1¼—1½-pound lobster per person

Robert Tristram Coffin, that consummate Maine man, writes in one of his delightful books, "A lobster still cold from his ten fathoms of dark sea should be plunged into scalding water before he has time to warm up and meditate and become mean and low-spirited and taste like a dull crab."

Mr. Coffin had lobsters right outside his back door, but those not so lucky should test a lobster by lifting a claw (a pegged one if you are cautious) to see if there is still plenty of life in him. If he makes no resistance and collapses in a limp heap, not even moving a feeler, refuse to have anything more to do with him. To be good eating, a lobster must be so alive that you can sense him moving inside his carapace. If you are fortunate enough to live near salt water, by all means fetch some to boil him in. If you must make do with tap water, add salt, 1 tablespoon for each quart of fresh water.

1¼-1½-pound lobster per person
1 tablespoon whole peppercorns
1 lemon, quartered
A large kettle of boiling salted water (about 1 quart per lobster is plenty)
Melted butter to serve with hot lobster, or mayonnaise with cold

Put the whole peppercorns and quartered lemon into the water and bring to a furious boil. Slip the lobsters into the water, one at a time, head down. Cover the top of the kettle with heavy brown wrapping paper, cut a little larger than the pot. (A supermarket bag, cut open, does nicely.) Place the lid over the paper and put a heavy weight on it to keep it firmly in place, and the steam where it belongs. (I use the largest black frying pan I have, upside down.)

After 12 minutes, take the lid off, reach in carefully and pluck one of the small side legs off the top lobster. If it comes away easily, and if it tastes right when you bite into it, the lobsters are done. In any event, they should be done by the time 15 minutes have passed. It depends on firepower from the burners on your range.

Drain immediately. Split each lobster lengthwise, take out the stomach sac and the intestine, but leave the green tomalley, and any roe, which is delicious. Crack the claws, drain off any water in them, and serve.

If the lobsters are going to be served cold, I hose them with cold water while they lie in the sink, then put them in the coolest place in the house until they are cold enough to refrigerate.

I serve my own Thin Cornbread (page 70) as well as Coleslaw (page 37), with the lobster.

Lobster Newport

Serves 4-6

In the days of the great mansions on Bellevue Avenue in Newport, Rhode Island, this lobster dish was a favorite, served as only one of 10 or 12 courses at dinner parties. I serve it as a first course, if I'm really being fancy; otherwise as the entree at lunch, along with a mixed green salad.

1 tablespoon gelatin
2 tablespoons cold water
1 cup hot chicken broth
¾ teaspoon salt
1 full cup finely diced cooked
    lobster meat
1 cup diced avocado
2 tablespoon chopped pimiento
3 tablespoon finely chopped
    scallions
1 tablespoon chopped green or
    black olives
Dash of Worcestershire sauce
¾ cup heavy cream, whipped
2 egg whites, beaten until they
    form peaks
Lettuce leaves, for garnish
½ cup mayonnaise, thinned with a
    little lemon juice

Soften the gelatin in cold water, then dissolve it in the hot chicken broth, but do not allow to boil. Stir well. Add the salt, lobster meat, avocado, pimiento, scallions, olives (if used) and Worcestershire sauce. Stir everything well together in the broth. Chill just until it begins to thicken, then fold in the whipped cream and the whipped egg whites. Turn into a lightly oiled mold and chill until firm. Unmold on lettuce leaves and serve with thinned mayonnaise.

NOTE: To unmold, dip the mold for a few seconds into a pan of warm water and immediately turn the mold over onto the platter. Shake it ever so slightly to loosen the contents. Or, if you prefer, turn the mold upside down on the platter and press hot, wet towels against the outside.

Scallop Mousse

Here in New England we have two kinds of scallops. The small bay scallop is delicate and takes careful handling; it is best sautéed or simply broiled. The sea scallop is much larger and has a hearty flavor; it is the favorite of people along the coast of Maine. Large as it is, it is still beautifully tender, and makes a delicious mousse.

This is a simple dish to make with a blender or a food processor and the result is impressive. If only bay scallops are available, by all means use them. Small is beautiful, too.

**2 pounds fresh scallops, large
 or small
2 cups light cream
3 egg whites, lightly beaten
¼ teaspoon freshly ground
 nutmeg
Salt and white pepper to taste**

Lightly oil the inside of a 1-quart form. (I use a form in the shape of a fish, but a round or oblong one will do as well.) If you are using large scallops, cut each one into 2 or 3 pieces, place them in the food processor and turn it on. Gradually add the cream and the lightly beaten egg whites. (If your processor is a small one, you may have to do this in two portions.) While the machine is still blending, add the nutmeg, salt and pepper.

To test for seasoning, have ready a small pan of boiling water and drop a small spoonful of the raw mousse into it. Allow to boil for a couple of minutes, then taste—and if more seasoning needs to be added, do this while the mousse is still in the processor.

Preheat the oven to 350 degrees.

Transfer the raw mousse from the processor bowl to the oiled form. Take the form and drop it on the counter 2 or 3 times to settle the mousse and eliminate any air pockets. Put the form in a larger pan containing an inch or so of water—a roasting pan serves very well—place in the preheated oven, and bake for 40 to 45 minutes, until the mousse feels quite firm to the touch. Take it out of the oven and remove from the water. Allow to cool slightly, for 5 to 10 minutes, then turn the mousse out onto a platter. If there is any liquid, blot it up with paper towel.

Serve with Lobster Sauce or a Sauce Aurore.

BÉCHAMEL SAUCE

2 tablespoons butter
2 tablespoons flour
1 cup liquid (this can be cream, milk, or half cream and half broth, either fish for fish dishes, or poultry or meat for meat dishes)
Salt, pepper and nutmeg to taste

Melt the butter in a saucepan and add the flour, stirring well. Remove from the heat and gradually add the liquid, using a whisk to eliminate any lumps. Cook over low heat, stirring constantly, for 5 to 10 minutes, until the sauce is quite smooth. Add the seasonings and blend well.

This is a basic cream sauce used in the composition of many dishes. You can double or triple this quantity at one time, but be sure to keep the same proportions.

LOBSTER SAUCE

3 cups Béchamel Sauce (above)
1 tablespoon butter
1 cup cooked diced lobster meat or cooked shrimp, shelled and diced
Salt and pepper to taste
¼ cup Madeira or sherry
Chopped fresh dill for garnish

Make the béchamel sauce following instructions in the previous recipe. Melt the butter in a small frying pan and sauté the lobster meat or shrimp. Add this to the sauce and cook briefly over low heat or in a double boiler for 10 minutes, stirring occasionally. Season with salt and pepper. Just before serving, stir in the Madeira or sherry. Pour the sauce over the scallop mousse, garnish with chopped dill, and serve.

SAUCE AURORE

2 cups Béchamel Sauce (above)
2 tablespoons freshly grated Parmesan cheese
3 tablespoons tomato puree or thick, reduced tomato sauce
Cream, if necessary, to thin
1 tablespoon butter
Chopped parsley for garnish

Prepare the béchamel and stir the grated Parmesan cheese and the tomato puree into the hot sauce. If the sauce seems too thick, thin it with a little additional cream. Just before serving, stir in the butter and blend well. Pour over the scallop mousse and garnish with chopped parsley.

NOTE: Both these sauces can be used with many fish dishes.

Parsley-Stuffed Tinker Mackerel

Serves 4

If you look out across Blue Hill Bay on a windless day in August and see great patches of ripples moving about, breaking the smooth surface of the water, you don't need a diving seagull to tell you that the mackerel have arrived.

I have a friend whose greatest pleasure is to drift in a small boat across the bay on a day like that, his line baited with strips of salt pork (he believes the fish should be well fed, too), idly pulling in the small tinker mackerel.

And when he comes in to his dock, I am there to meet him, and he fills my basket with small, shining, still wriggling fish.

**10-12 small fresh mackerel,
   cleaned and heads cut off**
Salt and pepper to taste
1½-2 cups chopped parsley
3 tablespoons unsalted butter
String, for tying up the mackerel

Sprinkle the inside of each fish with a little salt and pepper. Stuff each as full as possible with parsley and tie string around each fish in several places to keep the parsley in.

Heat the butter in a large frying pan. (We use a big black iron one, called a "spider" in New England.) When the butter is light brown, lay the fish in the pan and sauté over moderate heat for 8 to 10 minutes, turning the fish carefully once.

Remove the fish from the pan, put on a platter and cut off the strings. Pour over any butter that is left in the pan, and serve immediately.

NOTE: Small, freshly dug new potatoes are the obvious accompaniment to this.

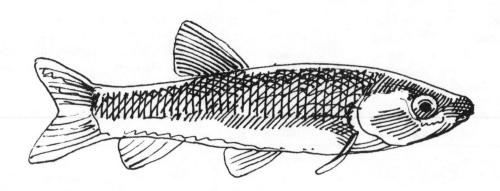

Fillets of Sole "Meadow Rue"

In the summers here on Blue Hill Bay, when our boys were growing up, they would spend hours fishing from the end of the boathouse dock, and would bring home delicious small flounder. Now the boys are grown and the flounder have gone out of the bay, and I make this dish with fillets of sole or any firm white fish I can find in the market.

The recipe calls for ripe tomatoes, but in our short growing season the first tomatoes of the garden are much too precious to be eaten any way but fresh in a salad. Later in the season, when we can gather them freely, we do use them in this dish. But in winter, rather than buy those poor pale things that pass for tomatoes in the stores, I make this and any other dish that calls for tomatoes with the canned Italian type, a quite serviceable substitute.

4 tablespoons unsalted butter
1 tablespoon finely chopped shallots
½ pound mushrooms, sliced
2 tablespoons chopped parsley
6 small fillets of sole or flounder
3 ripe tomatoes, peeled, seeded and chopped
1 cup dry white wine
½ cup fish stock or clam broth, homemade or bottled
2 tablespoons Béchamel Sauce (see page 43)
1 teaspoon tomato paste
½ teaspoon salt
Dash of cayenne pepper
4 tablespoons heavy cream, whipped

Put 2 tablespoons of the butter in a large, flat saucepan and add the shallots, mushrooms and half the parsley. Lay the fish fillets on top. Spread the chopped tomatoes and the rest of the parsley over the fish. Add the white wine and fish stock or clam broth. Cover the pan with a piece of wax paper cut to fit, bring to a boil and then immediately turn the heat down and allow to simmer for 8 to 10 minutes, depending on the thickness of the fish.

Remove the fillets carefully to a heatproof serving dish, draining the juice from them back into the pan, and cook the liquid until reduced to one-third its original quantity. Add the cream sauce and tomato paste, stirring well to blend, and salt and cayenne pepper. Taste for seasoning. Bit by bit, stir in the remaining butter. Pour the sauce over the fish. Now the dish is ready for the last step.

Just before serving, preheat the broiler.

Top the dish with the whipped cream, spreading it on top of the sauce, and slip under the very hot broiler for a minute or two to glaze. Watch carefully, and take out just at the point when the whipped cream has turned a nice golden color.

Salmon with Sorrel Sauce

Among fish, I give priority to the salmon. It is the first fish I remember from childhood. I can still see my Norwegian grandfather, rubber-booted, standing on a rock in midstream, his fishing rod suddenly bending in an arc, and a short while later the beautiful silvery fish being carried into the kitchen. If it was a large fish, part of it was sent away to be smoked, to be served at late evening meals with scrambled eggs and small boiled potatoes. The rest of it would be poached in the long fish cooker over the crackling wood-stove fire, to be served for dinner that evening, swimming in melted butter and chopped parsley and accompanied by cucumber salad.

When we eat the first Atlantic salmon of the season on the Fourth of July (along with the first early peas), I am usually content to serve it with melted butter and parsley, but I sometimes serve it with a sorrel sauce—and you may like to, too.

The crème fraîche gives a special flavor to this sauce. If you cannot purchase it locally, it is very easy to make, following the directions given here. Remember, though, to start this task a couple of days ahead of the time you plan to serve the salmon.

2½-3 pound piece fresh salmon, center cut if possible

COURT-BOUILLON:
1 cup dry white wine
2 cups water
½ lemon
Bouquet garni of fresh or dried herbs tied in cheesecloth

SORREL SAUCE:
Generous handful of sorrel leaves, washed, stems removed and leaves torn into pieces
Reduced court-bouillon
½ cup Crème Fraîche (see following recipe)

Poach the salmon in the court-bouillon for 25 to 30 minutes. There is a method that says you should count 10 minutes of cooking time for every inch of thickness. Test for doneness by poking a knife into the thickest part. If the flesh is opaque and comes away from the bone, it is done. Remove the fish from the liquid, place on a platter, and carefully take off the top skin. Keep the salmon warm while you make the sauce.

Strain the court-bouillon into a pot and reduce over high heat until there is a scant cup left. Lower the heat slightly, add the sorrel leaves to the pot and wilt them for about 5 minutes, stirring to separate the leaves. Remove from the heat and add the crème fraîche, stirring it well into the sorrel. Pour the sauce over the fish and serve.

CRÈME FRAÎCHE

1 cup heavy cream
2 tablespoons buttermilk

Put the cup of heavy cream in a jar with a top, add the buttermilk, give it a good shake and allow to stand at room temperature for at least 24 hours. (I give it a couple of shakes during the day.) Refrigerate for 24 hours before using.

Codfish Cakes

In the old days before refrigeration, codfish was salted to preserve it. It turned out to be so good and so useful that people have been using it ever since. You can still find it in the traditional small wooden boxes. Obviously, because it is heavily salted, it must be freshened before being used. There are two ways of doing this:

1. Place the fish on a couple of wooden spoons or a small rack in a large kettle of water. If the cod has skin on one side, the side without the skin should be downward, so that the salt will sink to the bottom of the kettle. Heat until the water is just barely warm, then remove the kettle from the heat and leave the cod to soak overnight.

2. Place the fish in a kettle of cold water and heat to just below boiling point. Discard the water and repeat the process with fresh water. Three changes of water should be sufficient, as you do not wish to take all the flavor out of the cod. Tasting is the surest way to tell how many changes of water are required.

After the fish has been freshened, it only needs to be simmered in fresh water, just below boiling point, for 3 or 4 minutes. Do not boil, because boiling makes the fish tough. When the fish has cooled, flake it with a fork. It is now ready for use.

**3 medium-size potatoes, boiled
  and peeled
1½ cups flaked, freshened codfish
1 egg, lightly beaten with
⅓ cup cream**

Mash the potatoes with a fork, mix them with the flaked fish, add the egg and the cream together, and combine well. Form into small round cakes and fry on a fairly hot, buttered skillet.

MAIN COURSES

I'm sure there was more flavor in the tough meats the early settlers ate—when they were lucky enough to bring meat to table—than in the specially fed and hormone-injected livestock raised for our dining pleasure today. If you are lucky enough to find a source of good meat that hasn't been laced with hormones and antibiotics, feel thankful, as our forefathers did.

Beef has always been a favorite American food—it's part of our English inheritance. But the consumption of beef has diminished in our time, and it's understandable. We find it too heavy these days. Oh, there's nothing like a big, thick, juicy steak when you want it, and the hamburger places still thrive, but for everyday eating many of us find beef too rich.

In Europe, if you go to one of the famous health spas like Vichy or Montecatini for an overhaul (it's just like taking your car for a spring tune-up), the first thing they do is take you off beef. It's chicken and fish all the way—and some veal, for Europeans consider veal light and healthy, as meats go. It's a pity that in our country veal has become so expensive, and that the raising and slaughtering of the young calves that provide it has become so controversial.

But we always have chicken. I mourn the scarcity of those nice small broilers that lend themselves to grilling, and are little enough to be served one to a person. And I wish there weren't a trend in supermarkets to cut up and package most chickens. It may be a convenience if you're in a hurry and only want breasts or thighs or even wings, but it is really more satisfactory to get a whole bird and cut it up yourself. It costs less, and you have the carcass for your soup pot.

You'll find recipes here for meat dishes that I particularly like, and you'll always catch me working on a good beef stew or a leg of lamb—but more and more these days I find myself thinking of the many different ways to prepare chicken.

Beef à la Lindstrøm
(GROUND BEEF WITH PICKLED BEETS AND CAPERS) Serves 4-6

In this day of ever-rising prices, it is useful to know how to stretch a meat dish and still have it tasty. I make this recipe and the Veal and Pork Patties (page 58) often, not just from economy, but because my family likes them both.

Beef à la Lindstrøm was given me by a famous actor whose forebears came from Sweden: Alfred Lunt. He gave me very specific directions for this dish, and I follow them faithfully, even to using a two-pronged fork to mix the ingredients. "Two prongs," he said, firmly, "never three."

1 pound ground lean beef,
** chuck or round**
½ cup cream
Salt and pepper to taste
4-5 pickled beets, finely chopped
2 tablespoons finely chopped
** onion**
1 tablespoon chopped capers
2 medium-size boiled potatoes,
** finely chopped**
3-4 tablespoons butter, as needed
Hot water, as needed
1 tablespoon whole capers

Using a two-pronged fork, stir the cream vigorously into the meat and add the salt and pepper. Then stir in the beets, onion, chopped capers and potatoes. Form into "hamburgers," about an inch thick, and let them sit at room temperature for an hour, "even on a summer day," says Mr. Lunt.

Brown the beef cakes in butter over a hot fire, turning only once. They should be crusty outside and pink inside. Remove them to a hot platter, add a few spoonfuls of hot water to the butter in the pan, add the whole capers, heat for a few seconds and pour the sauce over the meat cakes. (Mr. Lunt advocated broiled tomatoes and an ice-cold bottle of beer to accompany this.)

Alfred Hitchcock's Steak and Kidney Pie Serves 8

Alfred Hitchcock was a great connoisseur of good food, and though he rarely put spoon to pot, he certainly knew what good cooking was all about. He did not want elaborate dishes, but he did demand the best and the freshest of all ingredients. The finest veal was shipped to him in California from a New York butcher, the season's first delectable small potatoes were flown to him from the Channel Island of Jersey, and I remember the day his wife, Alma, who was under five feet tall, came staggering in with a fresh salmon almost her size. It had just been flown in from Scotland and she had gone to the airport to fetch it. Alma Hitchcock herself was an excellent cook, made the lightest cheese soufflé I have ever tasted, and a delicious steak and kidney pie. Here is the recipe for the latter, as given to me by Mr. Hitchcock in his own words.

I wouldn't think of rewriting The Master, but the use of Crisco to brown the meat is arbitrary. I myself use peanut or corn oil. As for the chicken stock, any good brand of chicken broth will do if you have no homemade, or you may use beef bouillon.

Because bought puff pastry is not available where I live, and I prefer to make my own, I use for this dish the same lard-and-butter pastry that I do for Cornish Pasties (see page 61). It does not rise quite as high as puff pastry, but has a texture that goes well with the contents of the pie.

Take one oval deep pie dish with a lip. This can be any size suitable for the quantity required.

Obtain from the butcher 2 or 3 pounds top sirloin cut 1½ inches thick and also one whole beef kidney. All this should be cut into cubes, each measuring about 1½ to 1¾ inches square. They should be floured and then browned in a skillet in Crisco—make sure the meat is browned on all six sides.

Now, place the meat into the oval dish with an upside-down egg cup in the center (this is to hold the pastry up). Dredge the meat with flour and fill the dish with some plain strained chicken stock (Lyden's is the best). Put this in the oven, covered by a saucepan lid, and let simmer for 2 or 3 hours in a moderate oven. Cook until the meat is extremely tender and will break apart with a fork (and) all the gravy is now a dark brown goo. Don't make the oven too hot, otherwise you will dry up the goo, which is the best part of the dish.

If necessary, add a little more of the chicken stock so that the goo is level with the meat.

Now get some puff pastry from the baker (any good baker will sell you a couple of pounds). Roll this out and lay it over the top of the pie, which has now become cool after taking out of the oven. Trim the pastry around the edge of the dish and for decorative purposes roll out a strip 1 inch wide and put around the edge of the pastry. If you have any of the pastry left over, roll it out and cut some leaves, or other fancy design and with a little water moisten them to stick these on the top of the pie.

Now, beat 1 egg and with a pastry brush paint the whole of the top of the pie. This will make it come out nice and shiny. Put it back in the oven until the pastry is cooked and is a nice, golden brown.

Incidentally, don't forget to make a couple of holes in the top of the pastry to let the steam out.

NOTE: The Master omits to say how hot the oven should be for the pastry. I like to start it for 15 minutes at 425 degrees, then, when the crust starts to get a little brown, turn it down to 375 degrees and cook at least half an hour longer.

New England Boiled Dinner

A boiled dinner is a basic staple in the country kitchens of almost every nation. France has its pot au feu, Italy has a bollito misto, Norway has a dish of lamb and cabbage with whole peppercorns called fårikål, and in Austria it is said that one may have boiled beef a hundred and two different ways. Basically, what it boils down to is a piece of meat cooked with vegetables and a good rich broth.

The boiled dinner of New England is almost exactly like the boiled dinner of Old England. Here, we use corned beef; there, they use a cut of meat they call Silverside, which is very much like brisket of beef, but with a finer grain.

In picking my piece of corned brisket, I always go for the butt end, which is leaner. Some people prefer to cook the vegetables separately, but I shall give you the traditional recipe and let you go your own way.

4-5 pounds corned brisket of beef
6 medium-size carrots
6 medium-size potatoes
1 medium-size yellow turnip
1 small green cabbage
1 small crookneck or butternut squash

Put the piece of beef in a large kettle and cover with cold water. Bring to a boil, then reduce the heat and simmer gently for 3 or 4 hours, or until tender when pierced with a fork.

While the beef simmers, scrape the carrots and leave whole; pare the potatoes and leave them whole, too; pare the turnip and cut in sixths; cut the cabbage head in sixths; peel the squash, remove the seeds and membrane, and cut in large, even chunks.

The trick to cooking a good boiled dinner is to have all the vegetables done at the same time. Carrots, potatoes and turnips take about 30 to 35 minutes to cook. The cabbage and squash will cook in 15 to 20 minutes. As you drop each batch of vegetables into the liquid around the meat, increase the heat so that the liquid continues to bubble.

To serve, place the beef in the center of a large heated platter, and surround it with all the vegetables and any liquid remaining in the pot.

NOTE: I like to serve with this a horseradish sauce made of grated (bottled) horseradish, mixed with a little whipped cream.

Red Flannel Hash

Serves 4-6

Mr. Webster defines hash as "meat chopped into small bits to be fried in cakes." The secondary meaning: "to make a mess of." Several heavenly messes come to my mind under that connotation, and a well-seasoned Red Flannel Hash with a poached egg on top is one. This hash is the obvious aftermath of what is left of the Boiled Dinner.

5½ tablespoons butter
1 medium-size onion, finely
  chopped
2 cups diced cooked corned beef
2 cooked beets, peeled and finely
  chopped
1 large or 2 medium-size boiled
  potatoes, diced
Salt and pepper to taste
¼ teaspoon allspice
2 tablespoons cream
Poached eggs (optional)
Chopped parsley for garnish

Melt 2 tablespoons of the butter in a large frying pan and cook the onion in it until it is clear and limp. Stir in the meat, beets and potatoes, add the seasonings and cook over low heat for about 10 minutes.

Preheat the broiler.

Put the mixture in a baking dish and dribble the cream over it. Dot with the remaining butter and place under the broiler for about 5 minutes, until the hash has a nice brown crust. Serve, if you wish, with poached eggs on top, and a little chopped parsley sprinkled over.

NOTE: This dish may also be cooked entirely in the pan, letting it brown underneath. It can also be made with left-over beef.

Turkey Florentine

I am not going to tell you how to roast a turkey. Why? Well, if you are of the generation that buys a turkey injected with butter (supposedly) under the skin, and God knows what else, I cannot help you. I don't like to cook meat that has been tampered with by anyone but myself, and I'm glad I don't know all the things that are fed the animals these days before they get to the butcher. If you are of the school that believes that a nice, plump, fresh, unadorned turkey is the thing to start with, then you need no advice from me, for you have probably been roasting that Thanksgiving turkey successfully for years. In my opinion, however, the leftovers are the best part of the bird and what to do with them is a game that everybody can play. Here is a recipe for using the noble ruins—and remember that when the carcass is finally stripped, it makes a lovely stock.

2 cups Béchamel Sauce (see page 43), made using ⅔ turkey or chicken broth and ⅓ cream

1 tablespoon of sherry or Madeira

⅛ teaspoon cayenne pepper

2 10-ounce packages frozen spinach or 2 pounds fresh spinach

2 tablespoons butter, melted, plus 1 tablespoon cut in tiny pieces

1 teaspoon grated onion

3 tablespoons freshly grated Swiss (Gruyère or Emmentaler) cheese

3 tablespoons freshly grated Parmesan cheese

2 cups cooked turkey meat, cut into 1-inch cubes

Make the béchamel, add the sherry or Madeira and cayenne pepper, and set aside. Partially defrost the spinach, break it up with a fork and put it in a saucepan with 2 tablespoons melted butter. Cook until it is completely soft and starts to boil. (If you are using fresh spinach, wash it well and cook briefly in only the water clinging to the leaves.) Drain the spinach thoroughly (see page 9). Add the onion and puree in a food mill or a food processor, then stir in 3 tablespoons of the béchamel sauce and set aside.

Transform the remaining béchamel into a Mornay sauce by stirring in 2 tablespoons each of the Swiss and Parmesan cheeses and cook for about 1 minute, just to dissolve the cheese. Add the cubed turkey to the sauce.

Lightly butter 4 scallop shells or individual ovenproof dishes. Divide the pureed spinach among them, leaving the outer rim of the shell or dish bare so the contents won't bubble over and overflow, then divide the turkey in its sauce the same way, placing it neatly on top of the spinach. Sprinkle each dish with the remaining cheese and dot lightly with butter. They may be baked immediately, or made up ahead of time, covered with plastic film to prevent drying, and stored in the refrigerator for up to 24 hours, if need be.

When ready to serve, preheat the oven to 375 degrees, place the dishes on a baking sheet and bake for about 20 minutes, or until they begin to bubble.

Parsleyed Leg of Lamb

As a change from a plain roast of lamb, or lamb flavored with slivers of garlic, try this way of preparing it. The parsley permeates the meat, adding to its flavor, and the green patch that appears in each slice as you carve the lamb gives a pleasing touch of color.

A 5- or 6-pound leg of lamb
1 cup finely chopped fresh
parsley
Salt and pepper to taste
2 teaspoons chopped rosemary
(optional)
½ cup sour cream

Preheat the oven to 450 degrees.

Lay the leg of lamb flat on a cutting surface. Make a dozen or more small slits or pockets in the lamb, using a small sharp knife. The cuts should penetrate well into the meat, down toward the bone. Stuff all the slits tightly with the chopped parsley. Salt and pepper the meat all over and place in a roasting pan. (Sprinkle with rosemary, if desired.) Roast in the oven 10 minutes at 450 degrees, then reduce the temperature to 350 degrees and continue to roast, counting 12 minutes to the pound for medium-rare, 15 minutes to the pound for well-done. For a rule of thumb, I count 1¼ to 1½ hours, no matter what the size, and it usually turns out right.

Remove the roast when done, put it on a serving platter in a warm place, and let it rest for 10 minutes before carving.

To carve, lay the lamb on its flat side with the small end to your left. Carve flat in the French manner in thin slices. There should be a small patch of parsley in each slice.

To make gravy: Pour half a cup of boiling water onto the drippings in the roasting pan. Scrape the bottom well to loosen all the good little tidbits. Stir in the sour cream, adjust the seasoning, and serve with the lamb.

Applejack Chicken

In the old days, here's how they used to make applejack.

A farmer pressed a barrel of cider, and let it get hard. If he wanted it a little harder, he threw in some sugar and let it work all over again. Then he closed up the barrel tight, and hammered the bung in, and set it outdoors, and waited for a long, hard freeze. And as sure as Vermont is next door to New Hampshire, the hard freeze came. And when the farmer was sure that that barrel was froze up solid, he went out with a long auger and drilled through to the center and drew off the pot of gold that was nestled in there: pure applejack. And he carried it into the kitchen and tasted it. And when he found that it was good, he gave some to his wife, for cooking.

A 3½- to 4-pound chicken, cut up
4 tablespoons butter
⅓ cup applejack, plus 2 tablespoons to dissolve the cornstarch
2 medium-size apples, peeled, cored and diced
1 medium-size onion, skinned and coarsely chopped
1 medium-size carrot, peeled and cut into 1-inch chunks
½ cup coarsely chopped celery
½ teaspoon dried thyme
½ teaspoon salt
½ cup chicken broth
1 teaspoon cornstarch
2 egg yolks
½ cup heavy cream
2 teaspoons lemon juice

Preheat the oven to 325 degrees.

Pat the chicken pieces dry. Heat the butter in a casserole until light brown, then add the chicken and brown the pieces well on all sides over medium-high heat, taking care not to burn them. Heat the applejack until warm in a small pan, then set it alight with a match and pour over the chicken. Scatter the apples, onion, carrot, celery and thyme among the chicken pieces, and add the salt and the chicken broth. Cover the casserole and allow the chicken mixture just to come to a boil on the top of the stove. Remove immediately and place in the preheated oven for 35 to 40 minutes. Test the chicken for doneness by sticking the point of a small knife into the thick part of one of the pieces. The juice that trickles out should be pale yellow, not pink. When the chicken is done, remove to a heatproof platter and keep warm.

Strain the sauce from the casserole by pressing the vegetables through a strainer. (Discard what remains in the strainer.) Dissolve the cornstarch in 2 tablespoons of applejack in a small bowl. Stir in the egg yolks and the heavy cream, add the lemon juice, then add the juices from the chicken and vegetables. Heat the sauce, but do not let it boil. Taste for seasoning, then pour the sauce over the chicken.

56 / COOKING FROM A COUNTRY KITCHEN

Applejack Pork Chops with Ginger

Apples and pork historically have an affinity for each other (the suckling pig has to have an apple in its mouth), and when you add a bit of ginger, you have something deliciously fresh and new. And a bit of applejack helps, too.

2 tablespoons butter
2 tablespoons olive, or other
    vegetable oil
1 small onion, chopped
1 clove garlic, chopped
8 thinly sliced pork chops
Salt and pepper to taste
½ cup applejack
1 tablespoon chopped parsley
1 tablespoon chopped fresh ginger
    root
½ cup veal stock or chicken broth

APPLE GARNISH:
Butter to sauté the apples
8 ½-inch-thick slices from a firm,
    tart apple, cored but not peeled
    (cut slices right across the apple)
Sugar to sprinkle over
2 tablespoons applejack

Put the butter and oil in a skillet, add the onion and garlic, and wilt until translucent. Remove from the skillet and set aside, but leave the butter and oil. Sprinkle the chops on both sides with salt and pepper, and sauté them quickly in the skillet, a few minutes on each side, until lightly browned. Heat the applejack in a small saucepan, light with a match and pour over the chops. Sprinkle the chops with the parsley and ginger root, then add the cooked onion and garlic. Pour the stock over and simmer 15 to 20 minutes, until the juices in the skillet have formed a sauce. If they boil down, add a little more stock. There should be about a teaspoonful of sauce per chop. Arrange the chops on a serving platter, cover with the sauce, and keep warm while you prepare the apple garnish.

Add a little butter to the skillet, put in the apple slices and sprinkle lightly with a little sugar. Cook over fairly high heat about 2 minutes each side, turning once. Sprinkle with 2 tablespoons applejack, swirl around the pan and serve the apple slices on the platter with the pork.

Veal and Pork Patties

This recipe, like me, has its roots in Norway. It is the zwieback and the nutmeg that give these small patties their special flavor. You may substitute beef for the veal, if you wish, but your patties will not be quite as light.

2 eggs
1 cup light cream
**10 zwieback (the plain, old-
    fashioned kind with the baby
    on the box)**
2 tablespoons chopped parsley
1 teaspoon salt
**1 teaspoon freshly ground
    black pepper**
**2 teaspoons freshly ground
    nutmeg**
**1 pound veal, ground together
    with ¾ pound pork**
4-6 tablespoons butter
Hot water, as needed

Beat the eggs slightly and mix in ¾ cup of the cream. Crush or grind the zwieback. (It can be done by putting them in a paper bag and crushing them with a rolling pin, or grinding them in a food processor.) Add the zwieback crumbs to the egg-and-cream mixture, then stir in the parsley, salt, pepper and nutmeg, and blend well. Gradually combine all this with the meat, mixing it all well together. Form into small, flat cakes, like hamburgers, but no more than 2 inches across.

Melt the butter in a skillet and cook the patties over fairly low heat for about 10 minutes, turning once. They should be cooked through, not pink inside. Remove the patties from the skillet, swirl a few spoonfuls of water and the remaining cream around in it to form a sauce, and pour over the patties.

NOTE: These are very good reheated, and also freeze well, when cooked.

Chicken Salad Princess Elizabeth

Serves 4-6

Once upon a time there was a fairy princess with a gold and diamond crown on her head, who went visiting at a famous inn in a country called France. "Ah!" she exclaimed, and her blue eyes sparkled with delight as she took a bite from the dish set before her, "c'est si bon!" (She was English, but she spoke French very well.) She called for the chef, and as he knelt before her, she touched him lightly on the shoulder with her fork and said, "Arise, noble chef! Henceforth this dish shall be known to all as Salade Princess Elizabeth."

The story does not tell us if she said all this in French, but it can be assumed that she did.

2 whole chicken breasts, skinned and boned
2-3 cups chicken broth, as needed
2 cups cold boiled rice

MAYONNAISE SAUCE:
1 large egg
½ cup peanut or safflower oil
⅔ cup good olive oil (French is lighter than Italian)
1 tablespoon lemon juice
1 teaspoon salt
2-3 teaspoons curry powder, to taste
3 rounded tablespoons apricot puree, made from cooked dried apricots
A little white wine and a little cream to thin the mayonnaise, if necessary

GARNISH:
½ cup slivered almonds, lightly toasted
2 dozen seedless grapes, halved

Simmer the chicken breasts in chicken broth until done, about 15 to 20 minutes. Remove them from the broth and allow to cool completely. When cold, cut the chicken into bite-sized pieces and set aside.

Put the egg into a blender or food processor, turn on the motor, and slowly, slowly drip the two oils in. After you have dripped half a cup of oil, you can start to pour a little faster. As the mayonnaise thickens, add the lemon juice, salt, curry powder to taste and the pureed apricots. Taste for flavor and consistency. If the mayonnaise is too thick, thin it with a little white wine and a little cream.

Now here is how to assemble the dish: Combine the chicken with the mayonnaise (saving out a few spoonfuls of mayonnaise) in a mixing bowl. Place a mound of the cooked rice in the center of a serving platter and surround the rice with the chicken in mayonnaise. Spoon the reserved mayonnaise over the chicken and then sprinkle with the slivered almonds; place the halved grapes at random over the mound of rice. Serve up *a dish fit for a queen!*

Gwennie's Meat Pasties

Makes 6 4-inch pasties, or 4 6-inch pasties

There is a woman in our village who is famous for the meat turnovers, or pasties, that she sells in her small food shop. Though she has lived in New England most of her adult life, she came originally from the British Isles, and the recipe for Cornish Pasties is right out of her own youth. In Cornwall, when the tin and copper mines were working, this was the lunch the miners took from home: meat, vegetables and pastry, all in one neat edible package.

Any good pie pastry may be used for this dish. I like to use this butter-lard pastry.

Our appetites not being as hearty as those of her Cornish forebears, Gwennie makes slightly smaller pasties that are popular here for summer picnics, both on land and at sea.

1 recipe Butter-and-Lard Pastry (see following recipe)
¾ cup diced cooked meat
1 small carrot, peeled, cooked and cubed
1 small potato, peeled, cooked and cubed
2 small onions, peeled and finely chopped
1 tablespoon chopped parsley
Salt and pepper to taste
2-3 tablespoons gravy, or a little stock thickened with cornstarch

Roll out the chilled dough (not too thin, as you don't want the filling to break through) on a lightly floured board and cut out circles with a cutter or a plate 4 inches in diameter.

Combine the cooked meat, carrot and potato in a mixing bowl, add the onions and parsley, and salt and pepper to taste. Stir in the gravy, coating the meat and vegetable pieces. Place 1 tablespoon of filling on one half of a pastry circle. Wet the edge of the other half slightly (a finger lightly dipped in water will do it) and fold it forward over the filling, pressing down well all around to seal the edge. Mark around the edge with the tines of a fork. (If you like, you can refrigerate or even freeze the pasties at this stage and bake them later. I like to at least partially defrost them before cooking.)

When ready to bake, preheat the oven to 400 degrees and put the pasties on a cookie sheet. Brush them with an egg wash and poke 2 or 3 holes in the tops to allow the steam to escape. Bake at 400 degrees for about 20 minutes, then lower the heat to 350 degrees and bake for about 20 minutes more, until the pasties are a nice medium brown. Serve hot or cold.

BUTTER-AND-LARD-PASTRY

Makes 2 9-inch pie crusts

2 cups flour
5½ tablespoons cold butter,
    cut into small pieces
5½ tablespoons lard, cut
    into small pieces
½ teaspoon baking powder
½ teaspoon salt
5-6 tablespoons ice water
Egg wash, made with 1 egg
    and 1 tablespoon milk, to
    brush on pastry

Put the flour, butter, lard, baking powder and salt into the food processor. Process for a few seconds until the butter and lard are finely chopped. Add the water and continue processing for 4 or 5 seconds until a ball of dough begins to form. Turn off the processor immediately. Form the ball into a disk and chill in the refrigerator for at least 30 minutes before rolling out.

Canadian Tourtière (A SPICY MEAT PIE)

Makes a 9-inch covered pie

So many French-Canadians came to Maine originally to work in the mills in Lewiston and Waterville and surrounding small towns, where they settled permanently, that even today many street signs are bilingual and the phone book resounds with names like Chabot and Chalonier, Paquette and Poirier—and that fecund family, the Dionnes. The French-Canadians brought with them many of their familiar dishes, of which the spicy meat pie called a tourtière *is one of my favorites.*

This version comes from a French-Canadian friend. In Canada it is usually offered at Christmastime, but I make it often all through the winter, and serve it for a Sunday lunch, accompanied by a green salad.

1 pound ground pork
1 pound ground beef
½ cup boiling water
1 small onion, chopped
1-2 cloves garlic, minced
1 teaspoon ground cloves
1 teaspoon cinnamon
1 teaspoon ground allspice
1 teaspoon freshly ground nutmeg
½ teaspoon salt
½ teaspoon pepper
1 teaspoon chopped orange peel
2 slices bread, crusts removed,
    cubed
1 recipe Butter-and-Lard Pastry
(above)

Cook the meat in a skillet with the boiling water, breaking it up with a fork, until it loses its color. Pour off most of the accumulated fat. Add the onion, garlic and all the other ingredients, stirring well, and continue cooking for 10 minutes until the onion has softened. Set aside to cool while you make the pastry.

Preheat the oven to 400 degrees.

Cut the ball of pastry dough into 2 pieces. Roll out one piece on a lightly floured board and fit it into the bottom of the pie plate. Spoon the meat mixture into this shell. Roll out the remaining pastry and use to cover the meat. Pinch the edges of the crusts together and brush the top with the egg wash. Bake in the preheated oven for about 20 minutes, or until the crust is lightly browned.

Chicken-Leek Pot Pie

All parts of a chicken have use: the livers for a risotto or a pâté, and the bare bones of the carcass for the soup pot. There are so many ways of preparing chicken: plain or sauced, creamy or spicy. There is no end to the variations. Here is another for you.

The leek is the national emblem of Wales and it has traveled well from their shoreline to ours. Leeks flourish in my garden. I use them in almost all soups and stews and they enhance the flavor of everything they are cooked with. Above all, they form a blessed union with chicken. You may like to honor Wales's patron saint by serving this dish on March 1, which is St. David's Day, but I guarantee you will find it hard to wait a year before serving it again.

Meat from a 6½-pound cooked chicken, taken off the bones and cut into manageable-sized pieces (about 4 cups)
5 or 6 leeks (enough to make approximately 2 cups when cut up)
2 cups chicken broth
1 large or 3-4 small carrots, peeled and cut in 1-inch pieces
4 or 5 small white onions, peeled and left whole

SAUCE:
3 tablespoons butter
3 tablespoons flour
2 cups chicken broth (or the liquid in which leeks were boiled extended with extra broth)
⅔ cup cream
½ teaspoon freshly ground nutmeg
Salt and pepper to taste
Dash of Tabasco sauce

1 recipe Butter-and-Lard Pastry (see page 61)

Clean the leeks well, cutting off the green part and the root. (You use only the white part for eating, though I often throw the green part into the stockpot for flavor.) It is best to split the white part vertically, almost halfway down, in order to wash out all traces of soil. Boil the leeks for 5 minutes in the chicken broth. Remove the leeks and set aside. Cook the carrots and the onions in the same liquid for 8 to 10 minutes. Drain and set aside. (Save the broth to use in the sauce.)

Make the sauce following instructions for Béchamel Sauce (page 43). If it seems too thick, add a little more broth. Combine the chicken and vegetables in a 2-quart casserole and pour the sauce over. While this is cooling, make the pastry and chill it for at least half an hour. Roll out the pastry to the size of your casserole. I cut a circular piece about an inch wide from around the edge of the pastry and fit it along the rim of the 2-quart soufflé dish I always use for this recipe. Then I cut a separate round piece, slightly larger than the dish, because the pastry may shrink, and put it on a small baking sheet to bake separately alongside the chicken in the pot with its rim. (This makes a nice crisp pastry lid that I place on top of the pot, when ready to serve.)

Preheat the oven to 425 degrees and bake both the components of the pot pie for 15 minutes, or until the pastry puffs slightly and takes on some color. Lower the heat to 375 degrees and bake about 25 minutes more. Pop the pastry lid on top of the pot pie and serve.

Old-Fashioned Boston Baked Beans

Serves 12

There was a time when I lived in New York, but frequently took the two-hour train trip to Philadelphia to visit my parents. I usually planned my departure in order to eat lunch on the train, since the dining car was put on in Boston, and I invariably ordered the same meal. Somewhere between Newark and Trenton the waiter would set down before me, on the starched white tablecloth, a small brown glazed pot of steaming hot beans on a thick white plate, accompanied by two ample slices of thickly buttered brown bread. It was the only time I really enjoyed this classic American dish, and it had to do partly with the solicitous attention of the waiter, and the familiar view of small towns and open fields, and far away through the haze the distant spires of Princeton University, as we sped on our clackety-clackety way. There was also a euphoric feeling of relaxation that came over me as I left the bustle of my busy New York life behind for the more leisurely and slightly Southern atmosphere of Philadelphia.

Now, of course, living on the coast of Maine, baked beans and brown bread are part of my way of life. Our local grocery store bakes beans every Saturday for those who are too busy to bake for themselves, and every March, at Town Meeting time, the supper that is served in the basement of the Baptist church features dozens of casseroles of beans baked for the occasion by the industrious ladies of the town.

In New England the favorite dried beans for baking are either the small white pea beans, sometimes called navy beans, or the Great Northern beans. There are variations on the basic ingredients that go into the bean pot. Originally the sweetener was maple syrup, but when molasses became popular, this was substituted for maple syrup. Some recipes call for mustard and some for an onion. Almost all call for salt pork. This is the recipe I prefer. The vinegar and mustard make a nice contrast to the molasses and give the beans a little zip.

2 pounds Great Northern beans
2 quarts boiling water, enough to cover beans in crock
1 tablespoon salt
2 teaspoons dry mustard
1 cup chopped onion
½ cup molasses
½ cup brown sugar
½ cup cider vinegar
½ pound salt pork, cut into cubes
Dash of cayenne pepper or Tabasco sauce

Put the beans in a large bowl, pour boiling water over to twice the depth of the beans, as they will swell, and leave to soak for 2 hours. Drain.

Combine the salt and the mustard and mix well with the beans. Stir in the onions, molasses, brown sugar and vinegar. Put half the mixture into a 4-quart baking dish or a bean pot. Add half the pieces of salt pork, then the rest of the beans, and top with the remaining pork. Add the cayenne or Tabasco, pour in water to the top of the beans, and cover.

Bake in the oven at 300 degrees for 6 hours. Check the beans from time to time, and add a little more boiling water if they look dry. The lid may be removed during the last half hour of cooking, if you wish a slight crust to form on top.

BREADS

Wrapped store-bread and Kleenex are two famous American staples, and as a general rule they taste about the same. I was recently in the kitchen of a friend who is not a cook, and she was delighted when she opened a cupboard and found half a loaf of store-bread still soft. "How wonderful!" she exclaimed, "I've been away 10 days and this bread is still fresh!" Soft—but not fresh, was my thought, and I shuddered to think of the additives that had kept it that way.

Happily, now, there is a trend back toward home baking, especially among the young, and more power to them.

One of my earliest memories is of waking up in my grandparents' summer house in the mountains of Norway to the fragrance of baking bread. The smell came drifting up the staircase to my bedroom, as I lay there contemplating the gastronomical pleasure before me. I managed to time my arrival in the dining room just as the round straw basket, with its snowy napkin enfolding the freshly baked rolls, was set on the table. Crisp, fresh rolls spread with sweet butter from a nearby farm, birch logs crackling in the fireplace—what a lovely way to start the day.

I find the baking of bread a delight as well as a therapeutic task. Modern mechanical breadmakers are useful as timesavers, but the rhythm of punching and kneading a firm ball of dough by hand can be a wonderful outlet for minor frustrations and when I put my loaves in the oven, I like to stand a few minutes to watch a loaf rise, heaving with the power of yeast, like the living thing it is.

All bread is a descendant of the grain-and-water pastes that helped stave off hunger in Neolithic times. This most basic of foods took a great leap toward beatitude when leavening was discovered, and since then has gone through endless modifications and innovations. There is an almost infinite variety of grains and flours to choose from, from darkest rye to purest white. There are recipes for breads that incorporate herbs and vegetables, spices and fruits. One early cookbook even claims that Louis XIV of France preferred a pumpkin bread above all others. *"Chacun à son goût,"* as Louis could have said. My tastes are simpler and my preferences lie in trying combinations of the many different flours and grains now available, rather than adding extraneous ingredients.

Certain breads have an affinity for certain foods. Who would think of eating baked beans without Boston brown bread? And there is always the basic, crusty loaf of French bread, which goes with everything. "A Jug of Wine, a Loaf of Bread . . ." and you have it all.

Boston Brown Bread

Makes a 1-pound coffee-can loaf

The classic recipe calls for cornmeal, along with rye meal and graham or whole wheat flour. I like to substitute semolina for the cornmeal, as it gives a good fine crumb and a firmer texture to the bread, so that it may easily be cut in thin slices, as well as the conventional thick ones. The quantities given here are exactly right to fill a pound coffee can two-thirds full. When baked, the loaf should have risen to the top. The bread can also be baked in two smaller tins, if you prefer.

½ cup seedless raisins
Hot water, for steeping raisins
½ cup rye meal or flour
½ cup cornmeal or semolina
½ cup graham or whole
wheat flour
1 teaspoon baking soda
1 teaspoon salt
½ cup molasses
1 cup buttermilk

Put the raisins in a bowl and pour hot water over them. Allow to stand 10 minutes to plump the raisins, then drain them and dry well.

Mix the dry ingredients in a bowl and add the molasses and the buttermilk. Combine everything and, lastly, mix in the raisins. Butter a 1-pound coffee can thoroughly, all over the insides and including the inside of the lid. Fill the can two-thirds full with the bread mixture. Put the lid on, and over the lid tie on a piece of foil so that no water can enter.

Place the filled can in a deep steamer (I use my clam steamer) or on a rack in a deep pot or kettle. Pour enough boiling water around the can to come halfway up the sides. Put a cover on the pot or kettle, and a weight on top to keep all the steam in. (I use a large inverted frying pan as weight.) Steam for 1½ to 2 hours, adding more boiling water, if necessary. Turn the bread out of the mold and eat it warm, buttered, with Boston Baked Beans (page 63).

Two thinly sliced pieces of brown bread, sandwiched with cream cheese and cut into quartered segments, make a good snack with a cup of coffee or tea or a glass of milk.

Norwegian Christmas Bread (JULEBRØD) *Makes 2 round loaves*

I call this a "tea bread" because it is slightly sweet, and yet not in the category of cake. Try a slice, not only for afternoon tea, but with a mid-morning cup of coffee, or at breakfast, a thin slice spread with a little sweet butter.

2 cups milk
¾ cup sugar
4 tablespoons butter
½ ounce (2 envelopes) dry yeast
1 teaspoon ground cardamom
6-7 cups flour
1 egg
½ teaspoon salt
1 cup seedless raisins
1 cup finely cut citron
1 egg beaten with 1 tablespoon cream, for glaze

Heat the milk, sugar and butter, cool to almost lukewarm and stir in the yeast.

Put the flour in a large mixing bowl and add the cardamom. Beat the egg slightly with the salt, add it to the milk-yeast mixture, and add this to the flour. Mix it all well together, then take the dough out of the bowl and knead well until smooth. (This is a fairly firm dough.)

Put the dough into a buttered bowl and turn the dough to coat its surface with butter. Cover with a damp towel and put in a warm place to rise until doubled in bulk, about 1 to 1½ hours. Plump the raisins in hot water for 15 minutes. Drain.

Punch the dough down and add the raisins and citron, kneading the dough until they are evenly distributed all through it. Form the dough into 2 round loaves, place on a lightly greased baking sheet and allow to rise again until doubled.

Preheat the oven to 375 degrees.

Brush the tops of the loaves with the egg-cream glaze and bake for about 1 hour until nicely brown.

Panettone

Makes 1 large or 2 small brioche-shaped loaves

For years I eagerly awaited the season that would bring from Italy to our country a Christmas delicacy called panettone. *It was partly the charm of the large, pale blue cardboard container, with all the Italian lettering, that appealed to me. Inside the box was a round loaf of slightly sweet, raisin-studded bread, light and delicious. In contrast to the heavy, rich fruitcakes that burdened the store counters, the pale blue boxes with their airy contents were a welcome relief. The only drawback was the thought of the long journey the bread had taken to get to me. So when Craig Claiborne and Pierre Franey offered a recipe, I embarked on making my own Panettone, with the help of a friend of Italian background. Now I make it all year round. It is especially good with morning coffee and afternoon tea, and is still light as a feather.*

3 tablespoons (3 envelopes) dry yeast
⅓ cup warm water
¼ cup sugar
½ cup dark or golden raisins
½ cup diced citron
3 tablespoons dark rum
8 egg yolks (think of all the meringues you can make with the whites!)
Grated rind of 1 large lemon
½ teaspoon ground cardamom
Pinch of salt
8 tablespoons butter, softened
1½ cups flour
¼ cup melted butter, for brushing on top of the bread

Dissolve the yeast in warm water with 1 teaspoon of the sugar. Put the raisins and citron in a small bowl and soak them in the rum, giving them a stir now and then. Put the egg yolks into a large mixing bowl and, whisking steadily, gradually add the remainder of the sugar, until the mixture is pale yellow. Stir in the lemon rind, cardamom and salt. Add the yeast mixture to the yolks and beat. Add the soft butter a little at a time, beating well. Add the flour, stir it in and beat briskly for 10 minutes. Push everything down from the sides into a mound in the center of the bowl. The dough will be soft and sticky. Cover the bowl with a dampened cloth and allow to stand in a warm place about 1 hour, or until doubled in bulk.

Meanwhile, preheat the oven to 400 degrees and butter the inside of 1 large or 2 small brioche-type molds.

Punch the dough down, and mix and knead the raisins and citron briefly into the dough. (I don't know what others do with the leftover rum, but I either put it into the dough along with the raisins, or, if the dough seems too wet to absorb the liquid, I drink it on the spot.)

Place the dough in the well-buttered mold(s), brush the top(s) with melted butter and place in the oven. Bake 10 minutes, then reduce the heat to 325 degrees and bake 35 to 40 minutes more. Baste with the melted butter several times while baking . It keeps the top soft.

If the bread seems to be browning too much, cover it with a piece of foil.

This bread keeps fresh for at least a week in the refrigerator; it also freezes well.

My Four-Grain Bread

Makes 1 large loaf

Since I claim this bread as my own invention, I was amused recently to read, in a history of the early settlers, that they made a similar bread, with rye and cornmeal as the ingredients. They called it "Rye 'n' Injun" bread.

1 cup white, unbleached flour
1 cup whole wheat flour
1 cup rye flour (dark, if available)
⅓ cup cornmeal, either yellow or white
1 tablespoon (1 envelope) dry yeast dissolved with
1 tablespoon sugar in about ¼ cup warm water
2 tablespoons butter
1½ cups buttermilk
1½ tablespoons salt
1 tablespoon caraway seeds (optional)
Egg-white mixed with water, or milk, for glaze

Put all four flours in a large bowl, or a bread mixer, and stir them together. Stir in the dissolved yeast. Melt the butter in the buttermilk over low heat, add the salt, cool slightly and gradually add to the flour, until it makes a nice smooth, but quite firm dough. Add caraway seeds, if you like. Cover the bowl with a dampened cloth and allow to rise in a warm place until doubled in bulk. This is a heavy dough that rises slowly, so it will probably take at least an hour and a half.

Punch the dough down, form into a round ball and put into a well-greased round form. (I bake my bread in an earthenware form, but it can also be baked free-form on a greased cookie sheet.) Brush the top with a little egg white and water, or egg white and milk.

Preheat the oven to 350 degrees.

Put the loaf in the oven and bake for about 1 hour, until hollow when tapped on the bottom. This is a firm dark bread and can be cut in thin slices, once it has cooled.

My Own Thin Cornbread

Makes 32 pieces

In our family this thin, crisp cornbread is a "must" with lobster, but it is equally good with chowders and other dishes. And because it is so thin, there are many fewer calories than in the traditional thick Southern cornbread.

2 tablespoons butter
1 tablespoon sugar
1 egg
⅓ cup milk
½ cup white flour (a little less)
½ cup yellow cornmeal (a little more)
1 teaspoon baking powder

Preheat the oven to 300 degrees.

Combine all the ingredients, stirring well. Butter an 11-by-16-inch baking pan lightly and spread the dough in it with a spatula. Bake in the preheated oven. After 15 minutes, or when the surface looks dry and the edges are beginning to take on color, remove the pan from the oven and cut the cornbread into pieces approximately 2 by 3 inches. Return the cornbread in its pan to the oven and bake 10 or 15 minutes more until each piece is lightly brown at the edges and resembles melba toast. Remove from the pan and cool before serving.

Connie's Branberry Muffins

Makes 12 muffins

A friend of mine here in our village decided that since bran is good for you and blueberries are delicious, there should be some way to combine them to good advantage. She was right. The result was— not bran muffins, not blueberry muffins, but Branberry Muffins. I love them, and have them for breakfast and have them for tea.

¾ cup bran
¾ cup whole wheat flour
½ cup quick oats
¾ cup dark brown sugar
½ teaspoon salt
1 teaspoon baking soda
¼ teaspoon freshly ground nutmeg
1 cup blueberries, fresh or frozen
Grated zest of 1 lemon
½ cup raisins
¼ cup vegetable oil
⅔ cup yogurt or buttermilk
1 egg
¼ teaspoon rum extract or
    ½ teaspoon rum

Mix the dry ingredients together, breaking up the brown sugar with a fork. Add the berries, lemon zest and raisins. Whisk the oil, yogurt, egg and rum together in a small, separate bowl. Add the liquid ingredients to the dry ones and mix well, but do not overbeat.

Preheat the oven to 400 degrees.

Fill greased muffin cups about three-quarters full, or slightly more, with the mixture. Place them on a cookie sheet and bake in the preheated oven for 25 minutes, or until the edges of the tops begin to turn brown.

Cranberry Nut Bread

Makes 1 average-sized loaf

There is a young couple who live just up the road from us and supply us with eggs and the comfort of good neighbors. We went to their wedding, some years back, and had a remarkable feast afterward, all done by the family. The highlight of that wedding feast was a cranberry bread baked by the groom's grandmother. It was sweet, it was tart, it was light, it had body, it was absolutely delicious. So, of course, I made up to Grandmother, and she graciously gave me the recipe. Here is Grandmother Drew's Cranberry Nut Bread.

4 tablespoons butter, at room
    temperature
1 cup granulated sugar
1 egg, lightly beaten
½ teaspoon salt
2 cups flour, sifted with
    1½ teaspoons baking powder and
    ½ teaspoon baking soda
½ cup orange and cranberry juice,
    mixed (if using frozen juice,
    dilute 2 to 1 instead of 3 to 1,
    as for drinking)
1 tablespoon finely chopped
    fresh orange peel
1 cup cranberries, coarsely
    chopped
½ cup chopped walnuts or pecans

Preheat the oven to 350 degrees.

Stir the butter and sugar well together in a fairly large mixing bowl for 5 minutes, then add the egg and the salt. Add the flour mixture alternately with the mixed juices. Finally, stir in the orange rind, the cranberries and the nuts. This makes a stiff dough. If you have a mixer with a dough hook, it is easier to mix the dough in that, adding the berries and nuts last, so as not to crush them too much.

Turn the mixture into a well-greased loaf pan, filling it about two-thirds full. Bake in the preheated oven on the lower shelf for 1 hour, or until a cake tester inserted in the middle comes out clean. (If you double the recipe, you can make 3 small loaves, which are nice as gifts. Reduce the baking time accordingly.) This bread freezes well.

DESSERTS

As a nation we are avid consumers of sweets. It is only as we become calorie-conscious that we scrupulously try to avoid those sinfully rich desserts, an inheritance from the Victorian table, when a lady's waistline depended only on the tightness of her corsets.

But there are many desserts, equally delicious but less amplifying, based on fruits and berries. Summer brings us rhubarb and strawberries (a favorite combination), raspberries and blueberries in abundance, and later come autumn's pears and apples, peaches and pumpkins, all providing the basis for pleasing desserts.

And if you devise a really rich dessert for Sunday dinner, or some special occasion, plan the rest of your meal accordingly, and do not overwhelm your guests before they arrive at the last course. Start with a simple soup, or first course, followed, perhaps, by a roast and vegetables or a grilled fish dish— and then go all out for dessert. Treat your guests to the indulgence of apple pie topped with a large scoop of ice cream, or a delectable strawberry-and-whipped cream dacquoise, all crunchy meringue and sweet cool berries. Live a little!

Apple Pie

In rural homes of the last century, pie was often served at breakfast, a good, hearty beginning to the day's work. A charming old friend of mine has told me that as a young boy he was sent away from his comfortable Boston home to work for a time as a lumberjack in the northern Maine woods. Breakfast was early in the lumber camp where he lived, and the men stowed away enormous quantities of food in preparation for the long day's work in the woods. At his first breakfast, one of the numerous pies on the table was passed to our young friend, who politely declined it.

"No mince pie, boy?" one burly woodsman asked. "No thank you, not for breakfast," he replied, passing the pie on.

There was dead silence at the table and a look of utter bewilderment on the man's face. "Well, when do you eat pie, boy?" he bellowed. My friend cringed, red-faced. By the end of the week he was wolfing down pie with the best of them.

APPLE FILLING:
5 cups peeled, cored and thinly sliced apples
1 teaspoon freshly squeezed lemon juice, sprinkled on the apple slices
¾ cup sugar
½ teaspoon cinnamon
¼ teaspoon freshly grated nutmeg
¼ teaspoon allspice
Pinch of salt

1 recipe chilled Butter-and-Lard Pastry (see page 61)
2 tablespoons butter
2 tablespoons milk or cream

Put the sliced apples in a bowl, sprinkle with the lemon juice, and use your hands to mix in the other filling ingredients until the slices of apple are well coated. Roll out half the pie dough and measure around the pie pan so that you will have at least an inch overlap of dough. Lay the rolled-out dough over your rolling pin and fit it gently into the pie pan without stretching it.

Put the apple mixture into the pie pan, dot with the butter and moisten the rim of the bottom crust with a little water. Roll out the top crust and lay it gently over. Trim the edges evenly and pinch well together. Make several holes or slits in the center of the pie to allow the steam to escape. Brush the top crust with a little milk or cream.

Preheat the oven to 425 degrees.

Put the pie on a baking sheet and bake in the preheated oven for 20 minutes at 425 degrees, then reduce the heat to 350 degrees and bake about 30 minutes longer. You may be able to see the contents bubbling slightly in the center holes, and the fruit is tender if tested with a skewer or a small knife. If the crust is getting too brown, cover it lightly with a piece of aluminum foil.

The pie may be served warm or cool, plain or accompanied by either a piece of cheddar cheese, or vanilla ice cream.

Deep-Dish Rhubarb Pie

Serves 6

Though rhubarb, or Pie-Plant as it is called around here, is horticulturally listed as an herb, to me it is the first "fruit" of spring, and I look forward impatiently to the fresh, biting taste of those pink stalks, pushing up through the barely warmed soil after the long northern winter. Rhubarb has an affinity for ginger, and I will hoard any ginger root I have to put into the first rhubarb pie.

3 pounds rhubarb, cut in 1½-inch pieces
2½ cups granulated sugar
Grated rind of 1 lemon
2 tablespoons finely chopped fresh ginger root (or substitute 1 scant teaspoon ground ginger)
1 recipe Tart Pastry (see page 76)
Egg wash of 1 egg yolk mixed with 1 tablespoon milk, to brush pastry
Confectioners' sugar, for decoration

Preheat the oven to 350 degrees.

Combine the rhubarb, sugar, lemon rind and ginger in a mixing bowl. Pile this mixture, in a high mound, into a deep baking dish. (The rhubarb will sink as it cooks.) Brush the rim of the dish with egg-milk wash. Roll out the pastry dough, cover the mounded rhubarb with it and trim to fit the dish. Press the pastry lightly down around the rim. Gather the leftover pieces into a ball, roll out, and cut out 2 or 3 strips about ¾ inch wide. Dip these in egg-milk wash and place all around the rim on top of the other pastry, joining the ends together. Make imprints all around the rim with the tines of a fork. Make 3 vent holes in the top of the pie and brush the pastry all over with egg wash. Put the dish on a baking sheet (to catch the drips) and bake 1 hour in the preheated oven. Dust with confectioners' sugar before serving.

Blueberry Dream Pie

Serves 6-8

We watch the blueberries all through June and pounce on the first to come ripe in July, then eat them all through the rest of the summer, in every possible way. We make blueberry pies and blueberry pancakes and blueberry pudding and blueberry cake. We even have two dishes in these parts called Blueberry Grunt and Blueberry Slump, and I assure you they taste better than they sound. I only draw the line at blueberry ice cream; I can't stand the color. What we don't eat, we freeze. Blueberries freeze beautifully. Lawris Closson up in North Blue Hill told us the easiest way. "Just freeze 'em as you rake 'em," he said, "leaves, twigs and all. Then in winter, when you take 'em out of the bag, just rub 'em between your hands, and the leaves and twigs come right off."

4 ounces cream cheese, at room temperature
½ cup confectioners' sugar
½ teaspoon vanilla
1 cup whipping cream
Baked 8- or 9-inch pie shell (see following recipe)
4 cups blueberries, plus a few for decoration
½ cup sugar
Pinch of salt
1 tablespoon freshly squeezed lemon juice
½ teaspoon cinnamon
2-3 tablespoons cornstarch dissolved in ¼ cup cold water

Cream the softened cream cheese together with the confectioners' sugar and vanilla. Whip the cream and fold into the cheese mixture. Pour this into the baked pie shell and smooth the top. Refrigerate.

Put the berries in a saucepan with the sugar, salt, lemon juice and cinnamon, and cook over low heat until just soft. Add the dissolved cornstarch and cook for about 5 minutes, or until it thickens. Cool. Spread the cooked blueberries over the cream cheese filling and decorate with a few fresh berries on top.

TART PASTRY

Makes 1 8- or 9-inch tart shell

1 cup flour
2 tablespoons sugar
4 tablespoons butter
2 tablespoons shortening
1 egg, lightly beaten
Pinch of salt
A little grated lemon rind
3-4 tablespoons ice water, just enough to bind

Mix the ingredients by hand or in a food processor and chill the dough for 30 minutes. Roll out the dough to ¼-inch thickness. Fit it into an 8- or 9-inch pie pan or pie dish and chill again for 15-20 minutes.

Preheat the oven to 400 degrees.

Cut out a circle of aluminum foil and press it gently over the pastry in the pan, then fill with beans or rice to keep the pastry from rising while baking. Bake in the preheated oven for about 25 minutes, or until the bottom of the pastry looks dry when you lift up the foil. Remove the beans and foil. Cool completely before filling.

Maple Syrup Pie

Serves 4-6

Maine people say you can't tell a Vermonter anything. Vermont people don't see why anyone should try. I think it started when Maine claimed that its maple syrup was as good as Vermont's, or better. The reply from Vermont was a deafening silence. I don't know which state this pie came from. Probably New Hampshire.

1 cup maple syrup (only the real
   thing is any good)
1 cup water
¼ teaspoon salt
1 tablespoon butter
2 tablespoons cornstarch
2 eggs, separated
Baked 8-inch pie shell made from
   Tart Pastry (see page 76)

Preheat the oven to 350 degrees.

Set aside, separately, 1 tablespoon of the maple syrup and 1 tablespoon of the water. Put the rest of the syrup and water in a saucepan and heat to boiling point. Stir in the salt and butter and remove from the heat. Mix the cornstarch with the reserved tablespoon of water in a cup, add to the egg yolks in a saucepan and beat well. Add the hot syrup gradually to the egg mixture and cook over low heat, stirring constantly until thickened. Allow to cool slightly, then pour into the baked pastry shell.

Beat the egg whites until stiff peaks form and fold in the reserved tablespoon of maple syrup. Spoon this over the pie, forming peaks with the back of the spoon. Place in the preheated oven for 12 to 15 minutes, or until the topping is golden brown. Serve at room temperature, or cool.

Hartford Election Day Cake

Makes 3 8- or 9-inch cakes

This cake dates from the 18th century and was popular all through the 19th century when election days were festive occasions, to be celebrated like miniature Fourth of Julys. It is not known what lady of Hartford, Connecticut, invented the cake, but I suspect that she was a politician's wife with a very special talent and that she passed out pieces of the cake at the polls.

This is a good cake to bake on a rainy or snowy day that keeps you in the house, for it rises slowly. It used to take more than a day to make, but with our modern yeast it's only a matter of hours. And while you are waiting for it to rise, you can always go clear your desk or straighten your bureau drawers.

1 cup raisins, coarsely chopped
1 cup currants, soaked 15 minutes
    in warm water, drained and
    patted dry with paper towel
½ cup sliced citron
6 cups sifted flour
1 tablespoon plus 1 teaspoon
    (1⅓ envelopes) dry yeast
½ cup warm water
1 teaspoon sugar
1½ cups milk
    scalded and cooled
1 tablespoon rum
1 teaspoon salt
3 large or 4 small eggs
2 cups light brown sugar
1 teaspoon cinnamon
½ teaspoon freshly ground
    nutmeg

Put the raisins, currants and citron in a small bowl with ⅓ cup of the flour, and mix with your fingers to coat the fruit. Set aside.

Dissolve the yeast in warm water with the teaspoon of sugar. Stir the rum and salt into the milk. Put the eggs in a large bowl and beat well with a whisk, gradually adding the brown sugar. Beat well and add the cinnamon and nutmeg. Add the yeast mixture to this and the softened butter, little by little, stirring everything well together. Now add the flour, little by little, alternately with the milk-rum mixture. Stir until the dough is smooth. Cover with a dampened cloth and set in a warm place to rise for about 1 to 1½ hours. (I put mine in the gas oven, slightly warmed by the pilot light, or you can set the bowl in a larger bowl of warm water to help the rising.)

When the dough has risen, cut it down and mix in the raisins, currants and citron. This is a sticky dough, quite hard to handle. Allow to rise again for 30 to 40 minutes.

Preheat the oven to 350 degrees.

11 tablespoons butter, at room
   temperature
Molasses to glaze the top

Have ready 3 well-greased 8- or 9-inch cake pans or 1-quart round pans, casseroles or baking dishes. Divide the dough among these, smoothing down the tops with a wet spatula, and allow to rise again until the dough is almost level with the rims. Bake on the lower shelf of the preheated oven for 30 minutes at 350 degrees, then lower the temperature to 325 degrees and bake for 35 minutes more. If the tops are browning too fast, cover them with aluminum foil.

When the cakes are done, glaze them with molasses dribbled over the tops and return to the oven for 5 minutes. Cool on racks (before turning out of the pans).

NOTE: The cake keeps well in a cake tin and may also be frozen.

Pumpkin Flan   *Serves 8-10*

I decided, one day when weight was being a consideration, to make a pumpkin pie without the pie crust. This is it: a pumpkin flan, and I am pleased to say that it has been very much admired. I think it is the recipe I am most often asked for. (I use canned pumpkin. It's much easier. I've tried it with fresh pumpkin and couldn't tell the difference.)

1 cup sugar for the caramel
3 cups cream, or half-and-half,
   scalded
2 cups mashed, cooked pumpkin,
   canned or fresh
⅔ cup sugar
¼ cup rum
6 whole eggs, plus 2 egg yolks,
   lightly beaten
½ teaspoon salt
1 teaspoon cinnamon
½ teaspoon powdered ginger
½ teaspoon allspice
½ teaspoon freshly ground
   nutmeg

Melt 1 cup of sugar in a heavy frying pan, stirring, until it caramelizes. When it is a good rich brown, but not burnt, pour it into a 2-quart round-bottomed glass or china bowl, tilting the bowl to cover the insides with caramel.

Preheat the oven to 350 degrees.

Mix all the other ingredients together in another bowl, stirring well to blend in the spices. Pour this mixture into the caramel-lined bowl and set in a bain-marie (a larger container, such as a roasting pan, with water coming at least 1 inch up the sides of the bowl). Bake in the preheated oven for 1 hour and 15 minutes. The flan should feel quite firm to the touch when you press with your finger in the middle. Remove it from the oven, cool for 30 minutes, then invert on a larger plate or serving platter. Wait 10 minutes and then remove the bowl.

This is pretty served with whipped cream piped around the edge.

October Pears and Ginger

Serves 6-8

Anjou, or Bartlett, or any good firm pears may be used for this dish. The pieces of pear hold their shape better if the pears are slightly underripe.

6 pears, peeled, cored and quartered (save the peel and cores)
2 cups water, or 1 cup red wine and 1 cup water
1 cup sugar
Juice and grated rind of 1 small lemon
½ teaspoon cinnamon
2 or 3 pieces crystallized or preserved ginger, finely chopped

Put the pear peels and cores in a saucepan with the sugar, water (or water and wine), lemon rind and juice, and simmer gently over low heat for about 20 minutes. Add the cinnamon and stir in well to mix. Strain the syrup and return it to the pan. Poach the pears gently in the strained syrup for about 8 to 12 minutes, depending on how ripe they are. (The cooked pears should be soft enough to be pierced with a fork, but firm enough to retain their shape.) When the pears are done, remove them from the syrup to a serving dish. Allow the syrup to cool slightly, then pour it over the pears and sprinkle with chopped ginger.

This dessert may be served chilled or at room temperature.

Apple-Applejack Crêpes

Serves 8-10 as a dessert

The story of Johnny Appleseed is one of the nicest American legends and, like all the best legends, completely true. John Chapman of Massachusetts was a ragged eccentric who believed that what this young nation needed, now that it was a nation, was apple trees and more apple trees. And so he wandered through the Ohio Valley all through the first half of the 19th century, handing out seeds and saplings. Bless him! I suppose he was our first environmentalist.

You may have noted that I have several recipes in this book that call for applejack. It's because I think applejack is a fine cooking ingredient, on a par with Cognac and much less expensive.

I'm a great one for making crêpes. They serve so many purposes. They can be used for a myriad of desserts and they can be used to enfold shellfish or meat or chicken, held together with some suitable sauce. They can be made up ahead of time and frozen plain, with a piece of wax paper between each one to prevent sticking, or they can be frozen already filled and rolled, ready to be put in a baking dish and popped in the oven.

When you make this dessert, I suggest that you flambé the finished dish in front of your guests. Very impressive. But not near the curtains!

CRÊPE BATTER

Makes about 20 6-inch crêpes

1 cup flour
½ teaspoon salt
3 large whole eggs, plus
    1 yolk, beaten
2 cups milk
2 tablespoons butter, melted

Sift together the flour and salt and set aside. Combine the eggs and milk and stir into the flour mixture. Blend in the melted butter. Let the batter stand while you cook the apples; the longer it stands, the better.

Lightly grease a 6-inch heavy crêpe pan and heat until a drop of water dances on the surface. For each crêpe, pour 2 tablespoons batter into the pan, tilt to cover the bottom, and cook until brown on one side, then turn to lightly brown the other side. Remove and place on a platter, or on wax paper, until ready to use.

FILLING

Makes enough filling for 20 crêpes

10 large tart apples,
    peeled, cored and cut into
    1-inch chunks
2 tablespoons butter
1 cup sugar
1 tablespoon freshly squeezed
    lemon juice
½ teaspoon cinnamon
4 tablespoons water
4 ounces applejack:
    2 to flambé the cooked apples
    2 to flambé the finished,
    filled crêpes

Make up the crêpe batter and let it stand while you cook the apples; or make the crêpes ahead of time.

Place the cut-up apples in a saucepan with the butter, sugar, lemon juice, cinnamon and water. Cook over moderate heat, stirring gently, about 8 to 10 minutes. (The apples should soften but still hold some of their shape.) Heat 2 ounces of the applejack, pour over the apples and flambé. Divide the cooked filling among the crêpes, placing a spoonful on each and rolling it up. Place the filled crêpes close to each other in an ovenproof dish.

Preheat the oven to 350 degrees.

Place the dish in the oven for 10 to 15 minutes, to heat. Remove from the oven, heat the remaining 2 ounces applejack, set on fire and pour over the crêpes. Serve immediately.

Strawberry Dacquoise (A MERINGUE DESSERT) Serves 6-8

Strawberry season invites so many good desserts, and as a change from strawberries and cream and strawberry shortcake, try strawberries in a dacquoise—a crisp, flat nut meringue. It's a good way to use up those leftover egg whites in the refrigerator and also makes a very festive-looking dish for a party.

6 egg whites (almost 1 cup)
1¾ cups granulated sugar
1 tablespoon cornstarch
¼ teaspoon cream of tartar
Pinch of salt
½ teaspoon vanilla extract
1 cup finely ground nuts (walnuts, almonds or hazelnuts)
2 cups heavy cream
1 quart fresh strawberries, cleaned, hulled and cut into pieces (save a few whole ones for decoration)

Preheat the oven to 300 degrees.

Rinse out a large mixing bowl with warm water, dry it thoroughly and put the egg whites in it. Whip them until they form peaks, then gradually add the sugar, mixed with the cornstarch, cream of tartar and salt, and continue to beat just until well blended. Fold in the ground nuts.

Butter and flour a large baking sheet well (or you will have trouble removing the meringues), or use a sheet of aluminum foil pressed absolutely flat over the surface of the baking sheet. Draw 2 circles on the baking sheet, using an 8- or 9-inch plate as guide. With a large spoon, or a pastry bag if you prefer, place the meringue mixture on the baking sheet, starting in the center of each circle and working out to the outer edge of each in turn.

Place the baking sheet in the preheated oven until the meringues take on a little pale color, then lower the temperature to 225 degrees and bake about 1 hour. (I sometimes leave them overnight in the gas oven with just the pilot light on, or in an electric oven on "warm.")

Remove the meringues from the oven, allow to cool for 2 or 3 minutes, then remove them carefully with a thin spatula from the sheet to a rack. (Don't worry if they crack a bit; the whipped cream will disguise the crevices.)

Whip the cream, adding a very little sugar if the berries are not sweet. Put a third of the cream into a bowl and mix with the cut-up strawberries. Place one meringue on a serving platter and spread with the strawberry-cream mixture. Place the other meringue on top. Spread the remaining whipped cream over the top and sides of the meringue. Smooth with a spatula and decorate with a few whole strawberries.

Summer Pudding

What's in a name? In the dead of winter, Summer Pudding conjures up visions of picking plump red raspberries and shiny blackberries, hidden clusters of currants, and blueberries growing on a sunny hillside. In England, where this dessert originated, the berry season is long and prolific. Here, where there is not that continuous flow of berries all the time, some may be frozen and kept until later varieties are in season. I was once served this dessert five times in one week, in five different English houses. Each time it was served with great pride—the best of the garden—each time it was delicious, and each time slightly different. Here is the version I use; feel free to improvise.

Combination of berries in season
Sugar, as needed
Slices of day-old bread, crusts removed

Take 1 or 2 cups of raspberries and the same of blueberries and of blackberries. If you have some red currants or currant juice, or gooseberries, use these too. Stew the berries briefly together with 1 cup or more of sugar, according to your own taste. Cook them only for 2 or 3 minutes, until they are soft but still retain some shape, then set aside to cool.

Line a round, fairly deep dish (a soufflé dish does very well) with slices of day-old bread with the crusts removed. The inside of the dish must be *completely* covered, sides and bottom, to contain the juicy berries. Fill up with the fruit, draining off and reserving some of the juice. Cover the top of the fruit completely with bread slices. On top of this put a plate which exactly fits inside the dish, and on the plate place a heavy weight. (A can of soup will do.) Leave at least 6 hours, preferably overnight, in the refrigerator so that the bread becomes completely saturated with the fruit juice.

When ready to serve, turn the pudding out onto a slightly deep dish and pour the extra juice over the top. Serve with cream, if you wish.

Indian Pudding

Recipes for this simple dessert vary surprisingly. Some call for eggs, some call for fruit, some call for eggs and fruit, and so on. I've tried them all, and I find the plain old basic Injun Pudding the best. It is traditionally made with Barbados molasses, which is really worth it, if you can find it.

½ cup yellow cornmeal
5 cups milk (2 cold, 3 warm)
3 tablespoons butter
1 tablespoon sugar
1 cup Barbados molasses
½ teaspoon cinnamon
½ teaspoon ground ginger
½ teaspoon freshly ground
  nutmeg
Pinch of salt

Lightly butter the inside of a 2-quart baking dish and set aside. Preheat the oven to 325 degrees.

Put the cornmeal in a pot with 1 cup cold milk and stir well to moisten the cornmeal. Now put in the 3 cups warm milk and cook over low heat, stirring well, for about 5 minutes, until the contents are smooth and thick. Stir the butter and sugar together and add to the pot, then add the molasses, spices and salt. Pour the mixture into the baking dish and then pour the remaining cup of cold milk over the top, *but do not stir it*.

Bake the pudding in the preheated oven at 325 degrees for 30 minutes, then turn the heat down to 300 degrees and bake for 2½ hours longer.

Serve hot or at room temperature with whipped cream or vanilla ice cream.

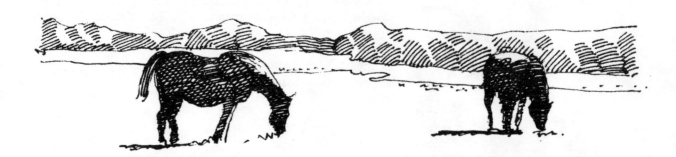